The
Outdoor Leader's
Handbook

How to plan, supply and guide an outdoor expedition for two to twelve people.

Best wishes,
Gil Gilpatrick

by Gil Gilpatrick

To **Dick Mosher**
My best friend and the best guide I know.

Library of Congress Control Number: 2002093565

ISBN 0-9650507-5-0

Contents

Acknowledgements

This book was made possible, and certainly better, through the efforts of many guides and other outdoor professionals who have shared their knowledge and expertise with me over the years. However, the following people were directly involved in this writing and are more than deserving of my sincere thanks.

Thanks first of all to my wife, Dot who has read and reread the manuscript and managed to get me to shorten some of my paragraph-long sentences. Many of the methods and techniques used in camping are a result of her ability to make things better, especially in the areas of food preparation and camp hygiene. Thanks go to my best friend, Dick Mosher who shared his experience and expertise in the areas where my own knowledge was a little sketchy. He also was a manuscript reader and his contributions certainly made this a better book. My thanks to Maine Game Warden Sergeant, Mark Warren, Chairman of the Maine Guide's Licensing Board, for his suggestions in the early development of the book and later for offering his considerable experience for the the chapter, Lost Person.

Thanks also to all of those unnamed people who appear in the photographs throughout the book. You are contributors as well.

Introduction

While this book should be helpful to anyone interested in the out-of-doors, it is especially written for those folks who have already accumulated a degree of experience and knowledge and are now ready to take on the responsibility of helping others, less experienced than themselves. The subjects touched upon are those that will help the leader to help others. There are also tips that I have discovered or "borrowed" from other guides and outdoors people.

Any time two or more people get together for an outing of any kind there will be (or should be) a leader. He or she may be formally appointed - a Boy Scout leader, YMCA leader, summer camp counselor, or church group leader. Or, the person could just be the guy or gal in an informal group of friends who is experienced and is just looked to for leadership. It could be Mom or Dad organizing a family vacation, or it could be someone who makes a living, or part of it, by doing what he or she loves most - showing people the places and things she or he loves. It is for the folks who find themselves in one of these sometimes unenviable, but always challenging and rewarding, positions that this book is written.

In over 30 years of professional guiding I have met thousands of people in the woods and on the waters of my state. Many were experts in their own right, and I have learned from many of them. I would never presume to tell them how to do what they do, but, as I gleaned tidbits of information and lore from them, I hope they have found some of my ideas and methods valuable and adaptable to their own outfits. I do know that a lot of them shared a common concern with me for the safety and well-being of people, especially children, on wilderness expeditions. Unfortunately I met others, not as knowledgeable and as well prepared.

Each year I observed groups canoeing our wilderness waterways who were sadly lacking, not just adequate camping gear for a comfortable, enjoyable trip, but also adequate safety gear and knowledge of procedures. It wasn't uncommon to see young teenagers with personal floatation devices (PFD's) buried under their gear where they would be unavailable if they were needed. Sometimes youngsters were observed paddling along, miles away from the rest of their group and their leaders. I don't think it was that the leaders didn't care about their charges. I think it was just that they did not have the experience and know-how to properly care for a group, and to recognize the dangers of wilderness travel. Apparently those leaders were chosen by whomever was available, not whomever was qualified. I will share two of the worst cases of irresponsible leadership that I encountered.

We were canoeing the Moose River in northern Maine. It was mid-afternoon and I had made the portage around Holeb Falls and was set up in a campsite below the falls. A group of young teens were portaging and setting up in a nearby campsite. As I watched I saw them bringing a boy down the trail on a stretcher. I immediately went over to an adult and asked what had happened and if I could help in any way. The man looked at me with kind of a blank stare and mumbled something. It was immediately obvious to me that he was drunk! Disgusted, I returned to my camp and let them proceed. I learned from one of the other youngsters a little later that one of the canoes had gone way ahead of the group and had gone over the falls. The boy injured his leg - they didn't know if it was broken. That evening one of the other adults (he seemed sober) came over to my camp and asked for help in evacuation, which I gave them.

The next incident was also a case of the leaders not keeping their young charges under control. This occurred on the Allagash River near Allagash Falls, a forty-foot, almost sheer drop. We had just gone ashore at the beginning of the portage trail around the falls. As I prepared to shoulder my canoe and start down the trail I saw a canoe coming with two young boys in it. They caught my attention because they were on the other side of the river instead of the side of the portage trail. As they drew opposite us, and started speeding up because of the swift current in the rapids immediately above the falls, one of them spoke up and said, "what happens now?" I yelled for them to get off the river, now! And they did. They didn't have a clue about the falls and their leaders didn't show up for another hour. The chances are that *this* falls would have done more than just injure a leg!

Safety is paramount for the outdoor leader and, while it doesn't have its own chapter, I have stressed it in each chapter where it is relevant to the activity involved. It is an old adage or cliché, but an ounce of prevention *is* worth a pound of cure. And the more you can anticipate at home, the easier things will be underway.

The outfitting and provisioning methods I have laid out are not the last word by any means. I have constantly changed, updated and tried to improve through the years. I also tried new products that came along - some were great, others were dropped after one try. I was never too proud to "borrow" an idea from someone if it made my trips better. By the same token, I hope you will use those ideas of mine that you like, discard the ones you don't, and let me hear about it if you have a better way.

On a wilderness vacation, a safe trip is the obvious priority, but reasonable comfort and enjoyment are important too. On one of his expeditions in Maine, Henry David Thoreau asked his Indian guide why he did not live off the land. Thoreau had an idealized picture of Indians traveling through the forest living off its bounty. An updated version of the guide's reply is: "No way am I going into the woods without supplies". His answer kind of reflects my philosophy. It is important to know survival techniques, but I'd rather keep them as a resource in case of an emergency.

Some folks enjoy gathering and eating wild foods and I certainly do not mean to belittle those who do, but I would strongly urge that the person responsible for feeding a group of people in the wilderness not depend on their gathering much of their food. Any windfalls along the way, like familiar berries in season, or fish, can be welcomed and enjoyed, but any initial enthusiasm for foraging daily for wild groceries will soon wane.

Where do you draw the line about what to take and what to leave at home? The answer is dependent on the type of expedition you are outfitting. A party on a canoe trip can easily take along more luxuries than one on a backpacking trip. However, if the canoe party decides it wants to make all of its portages in just one or two trips, then many of the luxuries will need to be omitted. You will see my choices in the chapter on Check Lists. I didn't exactly run an austere trip, but I feel we moved efficiently and the burden was not overwhelming.

There are subjects of vital interest to the outdoor leader that I have purposely not covered in much depth. That does not in any way minimize the importance of those subjects. They deserve a more thorough study than would be possible in a book such as this. A couple of examples are wilderness medicine and wilderness navigation, or map and compass. There are several good books available covering those subjects in much more depth than would be possible in this book. I feel the outdoor person should already have mastered these things before leading and taking care of others in an outdoor situation.

The old-time guide in Maine was more of a servant than anything else. He paddled the canoe for his sports while they sat idly in the bottom of the canoe fishing or watching the passing scenery. He all but aimed the gun, for the sport hunter, at the animal he wished to shoot. The sports told him what they wanted to do and he did his best to do it regardless of how he felt about it. Today's guide is more a teacher; he or she shows the guest how to paddle rather then providing all the paddle power. The hunter's skill is checked out and suggestions made if appropriate, but then the guide has to hope that the suggestions and instructions are followed. The guide makes decisions that will ensure the safety of the guests regardless of whether it is a popular decision or not. In some respects the modern guide has a harder job then his old-time predecessors because he is still responsible for the guest's well being, but often has to look out for them in a hands-off manner.

Some old time outdoorsmen understood the teacher role as evidenced by what Ernest Thompson Seton wrote in 1912 in his book, *The Book of Woodcraft.*

"Not long ago a benevolent rich man, impressed with this idea [taking people into the wilderness], chartered a steamer and took some hundreds of slum boys up to the Catskills for a day in the woods. They were duly landed and told to "go now and have a glorious time." It was like gathering up a net full of catfish and throwing them into the woods, saying, "Go have a glorious time."

The boys sulked around and sullenly disappeared. An hour later, on being looked up, they were found in groups under bushes, smoking cigarettes, shooting "craps," and playing cards - the only things they knew.

Thus the well-meaning rich man learned that it is not enough to take men outdoors. We must also teach them to enjoy it."

I'm not sure if this was a true story or one Seton made up to illustrate his point. No matter, it is as true now, early in the twenty-first century as it was at the beginning of the twentieth. The leader must not only provide for the physical things to make for a comfortable trip, but also should teach people how to obtain the maximum enjoyment of their wilderness adventure. When asked what that mournful call out on the lake was, don't simply answer "loon," but tell something about it. A few facts about the loon, like that it cannot walk on land or that it can dive hundreds of feet below the surface for food. All of those things about the out-of-doors that fascinate you will fascinate them as well.

It would be impossible in a book such as this to cover in detail all of the various activities that an outdoor leader might want to become involved in. However, the basics of leadership are the same whatever it is. For the person looking to guide professionally the best advice I can give is to find a niche where you are comfortable and then promote it to the best of your ability and resources. In my opinion the opportunities for guiding recreational activities will increase markedly in the future while those in the consumptive sports, such as hunting and fishing, will decline. There are several unusual guiding activities already and for sure there will be some in the future that we have not even thought about at the time of this writing.

Here are a few examples of a guide finding a comfortable and interesting niche. A young guide does real well taking people out on moose watches. He has a number of favorite places and can almost always deliver a photogenic moose for the eager watchers. Another has developed an interest in llamas and is offering llama pack trips through the back country. Packing by horseback is usually thought of as a western activity, but it is also done by one entrepreneur right here in Maine. Some guides specialize in snowmobiling activities to supply income during the long, slow winter months. The list could go on and for sure there are many that I have not heard of. The point being, if you have an interest, then there probably are others out there with the same interest, or would have if they knew about it.

As an outdoor leader, even for a short period of time, you are an authority, host, medic, teacher and companion, as well as a wilderness guide. In showing your people a good time, you'll also show them how to be responsible for themselves-and for their environment - and to appreciate the natural beauty that is still ours to enjoy. An important responsibility rests upon the shoulders of outdoor leaders, especially leaders of young people on wilderness adventures. And if they do their job well, the future of our remaining wilderness areas is assured.

Provisioning the Trip

Early wilderness travelers had two choices to provision themselves. They could live off the land or take very basic foods with them. Most chose a combination of these choices. The take-along food provided the barest of sustenance, and fish and game filled their bellies when the opportunity presented itself. Remember, these people, Indian or white, did not have the food choices available from the modern super market. Most times the take-along food was chosen to allow rapid travel, avoiding the valuable time it would take to search for food.

The voyageurs who canoed for a living in the fur trade had gigantic appetites. Records show their daily ration was 10 pounds of salmon, 15 pounds of whitefish, or three pounds of pemmican. I assume this was for the entire crew of one canoe. This is still a lot of food, but these traders expended a huge amount of energy, paddling 18 hours a day, with 60 strokes per minute. Amazingly, they made their portages at a trot, carrying two and even three 90-pound bundles at a time.

Lest you yearn for the "good old days," read the following

quote from H. M. Robinson's *The Great Fur Land: or Sketches of Life in the Hudson's Bay Territory*, published in 1879:
…take the scrapings from the driest outside corner of a very stale piece of cold roast beef, add to it lumps of tallowy, rancid fat, then garnish all with long human hairs, on which string pieces, like beads upon a necklace [I assume this referred to head-lice nits], and short hairs of dogs or oxen, or both, and you have a fair imitation of common pemmican. Indeed, the presence of hair in the food has suggested the inquiry whether the hair on the buffaloes from which the pemmican is made does not grow on the inside of the skin. The abundance of small stones or pebbles in pemmican also indicates the discovery of a new buffalo diet heretofore unknown to naturalists.

One thing you can say about the provisioning in the "good old days" is that it was kept simple: a bag of pemmican or a side of bacon and a bag of beans was all the planning required.

The modern outdoor leader has many practical choices and it is a good thing too. The modern guest does not expect to spend several days afield eating nothing but bacon and beans. This chapter will not give you a wide variety of choices of foods to take because I have not compiled a list of what others do. What it will give you is what I have found to be successful, and a way to organize and pack it. I encourage you to consider what you eat at home and find ways, if possible, to use that menu in an outdoor setting. That is how my menus got started. There are books on the market that list a variety of outdoor recipes that bear looking at. Read, and adapt the things that appeal to you and fit your situation.

The Menu and Shopping List

"How do you know what to take for food?" "How do you know how much food to take?" One or both of these questions come to mind when one contemplates provisioning an outdoor expedition. It *is* the hardest part of putting together the array of things that are needed, but it can be made manageable when the task is broken down to a day-by-day, meal-by-meal basis. This breakdown of tasks takes care of the "what" (menu) and the "how much" (list).

The outdoor leader planning for his or her own family or

friends has first-hand knowledge of the likes and dislikes, as well as the quantities likely to be consumed. Planning food for a group of strangers is not so easy. You must depend on good judgment and common sense, and draw on any experience you may have. The old saying "You can't please 'em all" holds true. You may have no way of knowing how many really big eaters will be along. However, if you choose good nutritious food that you like, and in a reasonable quantity, most people will be happy and satisfied. If you try to poll the group and come up with a menu to please everyone, the job becomes impossible.

I half-jokingly tell people that I take food that *I* like; that way I'm sure at least *one* person on the trip will be satisfied. This gets me a dirty look from my wife. Still, unless you have unusual tastes in food it is reasonable to assume that others will like your menu, at least to some degree. Don't worry about trying to serve everyone's favorites, but be sure to find out if anyone has problems with certain foods. If so, it can be serious if you don't learn about it ahead of time.

We had a man on a trip once who told us he was allergic to peanuts and peanut oil. At first I thought this was no problem. We wouldn't give him any peanut butter or peanuts. Then my wife and I started reading labels of foods that we regularly used. A lot of them, including candy bars, said something to the effect that the product contained peanut oil or some other oil. Those products had to be eliminated from the menu because we couldn't determine that the oil it contained was not peanut oil. We either changed the menu, where practical, or we took along a substitute item for the allergic person. The problem was so acute that we even had to be careful that knives that had been used in peanut butter (a staple for lunches) were not used by the allergic person until they were thoroughly washed.

Menu: The first step in the provisioning process is to prepare a menu like mine shown on Pages 10 and 11. The menu will handle any number of people; the quantities are adjusted on the shopping list to accommodate the size of the group. Most packaged items seem to be prepared for four people, so I used quanti-

Menus

Trip #: _____ *Dates:* _____ *Number of people:* _____

_{Day}   *Suppers*

_____ **First day:** Hot dogs, rolls, chips, onions, fresh carrots, mustard, relish, soft drink, cookies, (Weiner roast)

_____ **Second day:** Beef stew, biscuits, soft drink, cookies.

_____ **Third day:** Spaghatti, spaghatti sauce, hamburg, biscuits, soft drink, cookies.

_____ **Fourth day:** Hamburg Helper, hamburg, vegetable, biscuits, soft drink, cookies.

_____ **Fifth day:** Barbecued hot dogs, rice, vegetables, biscuits, soft drink, cookies.

_____ **Sixth day:** Macaroni and cheese, vegetable, stuffing, biscuits, soft drink, cookies.

_____ **Seventh day:** Hamburg Helper, hamburg, vegetable, biscuits, soft drink, cookies.

_____ **Alternate:** Canned ham, scalloped potatoes, vegetable, biscuits, soft drink, cookies.

_____ **Alternate:** Hamburger Helper (third flavor), Hamburg, vegetable, biscuits, soft drink, cookies.

Fishing: Fish chowder, biscuits, soft drink, cookies. (Canned milk, dried milk, potatoes, corn)

Snacks

1. Extra biscuit mix and season mix for possible fruit cobbler.
2. Cakes, etc. one or 2 for each trip
3. GORP or other snack for mid morning, 1 each day.

Recipes:

1 1\2 cups macaroni for ea. 2 people	1 can evaporated milk
1 TBS butter	1 TBS flour
1/2 tsp salt	1/4 tsp pepper
1/4 cup grated onion	1 cheese for ea 4 people

Photo 1 - **This menu would handle any number of people for up to nine days. My usual trips were for seven days.**

ties for four, eight or twelve people. For example, if there were six in the group I bought food for eight. This is not a universal policy for all items, but just a rule of thumb to go by when in doubt. You err to the side of too much rather than too little.

I like to write in the days of the month on the menu. I carry it

---

Breakfast and lunch

Breakfasts:

_____Pancakes, ham, with butter and syrup, coffee, hot chocolate.

_____Eggs, ham, biscuits with butter and jam, coffee, hot choclolate

_____Oatmeal, dried milk, raisens, biscuits, butter,coffee, hot chocolate.

_____Pancakes, Eggs, with butter, syrup, coffee, hot chocloate

_____Oatmeal, dried milk, raisens, biscuits, butter,coffee, hot chocolate.

_____Pancakes, ham, with butter and syrup, coffee, hot chocolate.

Lunches:

_____Lunch A: Bread, crackers, peanut butter, soft drink, candy.

_____Lunch B: Bread, crackers, cheese, soft drink, candy.

_____Lunch C: Bread, crackers, meat spread, soft drink, candy.

(All lunch items offered at once each day.)

Photo 2 - **The reverse side of the menu.**

with me on the trip, and it helps me keep track of the date. It is easy to remember what was eaten the day before. Keeping track of the date may not seem important or in keeping with the carefree spirit of the outdoor adventure you may be leading, but the leader isn't afforded the luxury of a carefree spirit. If your group is scheduled to meet transportation, get back to their job, or some other obligation, then it is your job to get them there on time. It would be embarrassing and troublesome to do otherwise.

In writing down items on your menu, try to think of everything in the food line that will be needed to put that meal before your guests. If you don't have things like sugar or coffee on another list, like the "Kitchen Box" checklist, then get it onto the menu so you won't forget to add that item to your shopping list.

I always tried to have a different meal for each evening of the trip. Breakfast and lunch, however, use the same basic foods in different combinations to give a little variety. Eggs with ham with one meal, eggs with pancakes with another, etc. Lunches are basically the same every day with the guests allowed to choose what appeals to them between the peanut butter, lunch meat or cheese or some combination of the three. Freshly picked berries can be incorporated into the meals when they are available. I found guests were often anxious to gather raspberries, blueberries or whatever, to help make meals a little more interesting. I always took along a variety of dried fruits, raisins, dates, etc. to use in the bread, biscuits and oatmeal to add variety.

I baked a loaf of Canoe Country Bread (see recipe on Page 59) every evening for the following day's lunch. Bread is bulky and cannot be kept fresh on an extended trip, but the bread mix takes up little space in the food box. Just so I didn't have to stay up late and do two loaves for large groups I included some crackers (Ritz or ?) to ensure no one went hungry at lunch time.

I used the same menu on all my trips, only using variations when it was necessary. After all, there were different people on each trip so the only people that saw the repetition through the season were my wife and I. The meals were things we liked so it was no problem for us.

I always took along a cake mix and some frosting. If someone happened to have a birthday on the trip we celebrated in style. A brownie or cookie mix was included as well. This was a good treat in the middle of the day if we were forced to lay over in a campsite because of weather.

Shopping List: Once the menu is complete and you are satisfied with it, make up the shopping list. This is decision time again, but a little common sense will let you determine the quantity needed of each item. As a general rule pre-teen children will eat very little. Teen-age children will make up for the youngsters and then some. Women will normally eat less than men and young men eat more than older men. If you are buying packaged foods you can find the number of servings on the label. For camping it is usually a good idea to allow half again the label amount.

Shopping List

Trip #: _____ **Dates:** _____ **Number of people:** _____

Suppers:
____Hot dogs (Ball Park & Reg.)
____Hot dog rolls
____Potato chips
____Onions
____Carrots
____Stew starter
____Stew beef
____Frozen mix vegetables
____Macaroni
____Cheese
____Canned milk
____Stuffing mix
____Vegetables
____Mix Veg. for stew
____Hamburger Helper
____Spaghatti
____Spaghatti sauce
____Hamburger
____Chicken
____Canned ham
____Scalloped potatoes
____Cookies
____Rice

Kitchen:
____Mustard
____Relish
____Drink mix (S & L)
____Biscuit mix
____Ketchup
____Grated cheese
____Salt
____Oleo
____Jam or jelly
____Veg oil
____Coffee
____Coffee-mate
____Tea
____Hot chocolate
____Sugar
____Snack cakes to bake
____Frosting
____Flour (for bread)
____Baking powder
____Cinnamon
____Pepper
____Muffin Mix
____Pam
____Honey

Lunches:
____Peanut butter
____Candy
____Cheese
____Meat spread
____Crackers
____Raisens & Dates
____1000 Island dressing

Breakfast:
____Eggs
____Ham
____Pancake mix
____Syrup
____Oatmeal
____Dried milk
____Raisens
____Tang
____Ice tea

For First Lunch:
____Drink mix
____Lunch meat
____Sandwich rolls
____Apples
____Brownie mix
____Cheese
____Lettuce
____Mayo

For Barbecued Hot Dogs:
____Vinager
____Tomato soup
____Worchestershire sauce
____Brown sugar
____Lemon juice

Snacks:
____M & M's
____Peanuts
____Raisens
____Other snacks

Other:
_____
_____
_____

Misc.:
____Brillo
____Detergent
____Paper towels
____Toilet paper
____Hand soap
____Sponge
____Large HD garbage bags
____Plastic freezer bags
____Toothpaste
____Razor blades
____Fly dope
____Bic lighter
____Flashlight batteries
____Film
____Stove fuel
____Fly spray
____Medical supplies
____Duct tape
____Motor gas
____Ice
____Chain oil

Photo 3 - This shopping list is ready made - only the amounts need to be filled in.

The shopping list shown has some items that are shaded. These are items that need refrigeration, but should not be frozen. Since I always did my food preparation at least a week ahead of the trip, I delayed buying those things until the day before departure.

That way I did not have to store the perishables in our refrigerator for a week or so, and it helped to ensure freshness.

It pays to have extras of some items. If you bring extra hot chocolate mix, everyone can have a cup after a long cold day in the rain. Extra biscuit mix takes up little room in the food box, but an extra batch would be helpful in stretching a meal that comes up a little short on something; another biscuit with jam or peanut butter will help fill up that hollow leg. Contingencies like these are impossible to plan into the menu, but are very easy to allow for. Peanut butter is a good emergency ration. Take plenty. Nearly everyone likes it so it can be used to fill out any meal or can serve as a filling nutritious snack. Not to mention a regular staple for lunches.

Once every item on the menu has been listed with a quantity added to it, make a list for other items you think you might want to buy for the trip. Such things as paper towels, toilet paper, dish detergent can all included on your shopping list.

Food Preparation and Packing

While meal preparation will be discussed in the Camping chapter, a lot to time and trouble can be saved by doing everything possible in the comfort of your home kitchen. The food preparation and packing for a week long trip took my wife and I the better part of a day. The reason is that we did a lot of the cooking and all of the repackaging in the convenience of our home. The main course for nearly all the supper meals were prepared at home and packed into the cooler and frozen as described in the chapter on check lists. As a professional guide I was interested in serving nutritious, enjoyable meals to my guests, and doing it the most efficient way I possibly could. Sure, I could have put everything together in the field, but why? The less time I had to spend in preparation while on a trip the more time I had to do extras like baking fresh bread each day and making biscuits for nearly every supper, along with showing them some beautiful country.

If you are on a trip in hot weather and your cooler is showing the effects of the heat, the cooked meals will keep from spoiling longer than uncooked food will. If you know the kind and amount you need there is no reason not to cook meats before packing them. An example of this kind of preparation is our spaghetti meal which was a favorite of nearly everyone on our trips. We cooked the hamburger (scrambled), mixed it with the sauce and put the finished sauce into a plastic bag to be frozen. When time came for the spaghetti I just heated the sauce, cooked the pasta and served it up with freshly baked biscuits and raw baby carrots.

I have been asked from time to time why I didn't use dry ice in my cooler(s). I checked into it and found, like most things, it had advantages and disadvantages. I learned that dry ice is 106 degrees below zero Fahrenheit (The home freezer is about zero). That means everything in the cooler would require a long time to thaw, which is not a serious flaw if you allow for it. But, it would mean that you couldn't use the cooler for perishables that should not be frozen, like fruit, eggs, or cheese. The most serious drawback, however, is the cost - it is quite expensive and not readily available everywhere. Still, it is something to consider under certain circumstances.

Many items from the grocery store are in very bulky packaging. A lot of space can be saved by removing the box and packing only the plastic envelope inside, or in some cases completely repackaging. Be sure to save any directions that may be printed on the box. Very often my guests were amazed as they looked over my boxes as we prepared to leave for a week-long trip. They couldn't believe there was enough food for 12 people for the week in those few boxes. This skepticism is understandable when you think about the number of bags it takes to bring home a week's groceries for a family of four or five. That's what repackaging and careful packing can do. Repackaging can also eliminate taking cans and jars on the trip. That means you will not have to carry them out, because you don't carry them in.

Another big time saver afield is to prepackage mixes you plan to use. I always bought Bisquick for my biscuits. I packaged it in two or four cup plastic bags, depending on the size of the group, and then in the field I only had to add sufficient water to whip up a batch of biscuits. No measuring required. Same thing with my bread. This also allows packing the biscuits or bread along with the meal they are to go with.

When you return from the shopping trip unpack the food and separate it into the various meals, breakfast items in one pile, lunches in another, etc. Then go ahead and do whatever preparation and repackaging that needs to be done. If the size of the group and length of your trip allows you the luxury of having a separate box for each meal the packing is simplified. At any rate, use your menu to pack the food in reverse order, last day in first, then the next to the last day, etc., working toward the top of the box in that manner. If you have to mix meals in one box, it will take a little longer and will require some concentration to get things straight. Very often when I packed mixed meals I found I had to take everything out and start over because of an oversight somewhere along the line. This is somewhat frustrating, but is time well spent because it is time you will not have to spend pawing around when you are trying to put a meal together in the pouring rain. When this happens everyone in your party will be crowding under the tarp with you as you try to do your job and still be patient and cheerful.

Traditional vs. Nontraditional Food: Here I mean supermarket food vs. prepackaged dried or freeze-dried foods available from camping outlets. Certain types of outings, such as backpacking trips, will demand a lightweight foods that will keep without refrigeration (cooler). If you are to lead one of these trips you have the choice of buying the prepackaged stuff for each meal and your meal preparation is done. However, died-in-the-wool backpackers have done a lot of research into buying lightweight (dried) food in the local market. It is less expensive than buying the prepackaged stuff. Check the library or book stores for information on lightweight meals.

My own experience with commercial freeze dried meals is somewhat skimpy, but what I do remember is that, while there was a variety of entrees available, they all tended to taste somewhat the same. This opinion was shared by others. I also remember that some people found it upsetting to their digestive system to switch from regular food to freeze-dried meals, or vice-versa. A leader who made multiple trips in a season, using only the prepackaged dried meals, might suffer a similar problem. Early on I decided that I would capitalize on the luxury afforded by canoe travel, that is the ability to carry along a sizeable amount of gear. This meant I could serve up a very close to home-cooked meals while afield. I guess it was successful, I did it for over 30 years.

There can be circumstances where even canoe travel will make one want to lighten the load a bit. Some years ago my friend Dick Mosher and I canoed the East Branch of the Penobscot River. Just he and I. We knew there were four long hard portages on the trip and so we tried to pack accordingly. We decided ahead of time that we were only willing to make two trips around each carry, then we adjusted the number of packs to make that possible. Do what needs to be done to meet the conditions of your trip and the needs of your guests.

So you don't forget...... Checklists

The outdoor leader is expected to make arrangements to move a group of people, and their gear, over miles of road, and to provide for their needs for several days in a wilderness situation. Further, to return home with no item unused except, hopefully, the raincoats, tarp and medical kit. My solution to this challenge? Check lists! Every single item needed is written on a list, and not checked off until it is packed away, ready to go.

Even before I started guiding professionally, I learned that if my outdoor wanderings were going to have any success at all I had to get myself organized. Otherwise I found my mind so occupied with the eager anticipation of the getting there that I did not concentrate sufficiently on the preparation.

I know check lists are not a new concept, but what the outdoor leader needs to do is make them almost a religion as he or she prepares for a trip into the woods. I have never thrown a list away. When I started using a computer it became a lot easier to keep lists up to date and make changes that are needed from time to time. Making those small changes as they come along is a lot easier than sitting down and trying to remember everything for a whole new list. And, after the first time out you will know that you have a list that has worked.

You may need special lists for each type of activity you have going, or you may be able to modify your existing lists. A list for a trip to a wilderness cabin would be a lot different from one where you would be camping out. A list of camping equipment for a backpacking trip would be quite different from that for a canoe camping trip. However, when the items that differ from one kind of trip to another are relatively few it may be easier to keep the items all on one list. An example of this is on my tool box list. I show a small chainsaw there along with the gas and oil to operate it. Many of my canoe trips were to an area where chainsaws were not allowed. When that was the case I just checked those items off (without packing them, of course) and once a checkmark was beside them my attention was not drawn to them again. If you look at my personal list, and then at the photo of me on the back cover, you will realize that I don't really need that shaving gear I have listed there. In the unlikely event I decide to shave off the beard I will be reminded to pack the razor.

Don't leave out items that may seem too obvious to include either. I always had canoes on my list for canoe trips. Who would leave on a canoe trip without their canoes? I included them because it reminded me to get out and load them - something I might otherwise put off till the last minute. And besides, it made my list *complete*. I admit I have never known anyone to forget canoes for a canoe trip, but I have known them to arrive without paddles. I also have known hunters to arrive at a hunting camp without a rifle. These things would seem just as obvious as the canoes.

Sometimes groups of items can be listed under one heading thus saving time and space if those items are always kept together. For example, on my personal list is the "Emergency Pack". That pack contains the items listed in the Lost Person Chapter. The list for those items are kept in the pack and needs to be checked only when there is a change or a replacement.

***Photo 4** -* **Silverware roll - made from a hand towel.**

My lists evolved over many years of continuous use, along with the evolution of my equipment. Their arrangement suits me and my methods. You may want to use them to get started, but eventually you will customize them to your own liking. The important thing is to get *everything* down on paper. Then, organize your lists so that checking items off is easy and natural for you, and as foolproof as possible.

Silverware is another item not listed one by one, but as a whole. Mine was carried in a role. (See photo 4) When I do up the roll, I know it is all there or I wouldn't have rolled it. With a different system one may want to list the silverware items separately to ensure there will be enough pieces for everyone.

My system consists of six different lists which are shown on the following pages (The "Kitchen Boxes" contains two lists). This doesn't include the menus and shopping list which were discussed in the previous chapter. Five of the lists are equipment I must pack, and one is my guests' personal equipment items which I expect them to bring. Four of my five lists are for the different packs that the individual items will go into. The fifth is a "Master List" which contains the name of the packs (already loaded from their own list) plus items which do not go into packs.

Individual items are checked off each list as they go into their appropriate container. By the time the morning of departure arrives I am down to the master list, having checked all items into their respective boxes. The master list is used to load everything into my truck. By disciplining my self to *absolutely not* check an item off until it is packed, there is virtually no chance of leaving anything behind. If it got down on paper, it will be in the truck.

It is bad enough to forget something if you are leading a group of friends or family, but if you are a guide being paid for your services it can be extremely embarrassing and potentially bad for

business. Even the best of systems can break down if you are not
extremely diligent. I remember one trip that I discovered I did
not have maple syrup with me. Since pancakes were the scheduled breakfast for two or three mornings this was no small thing.
Here's how it happened. As I went over my shopping list I checked
off the syrup because I knew we had enough in the refrigerator
and so I didn't need to buy any. What I should have done, and
what I did thereafter, was to set the syrup out where it would be
with the other food items as I prepared and packed them. I vio-
lated my own system by checking something off before it was
packed.

Review your lists often for possible additions and deletions.
Watch for items that never get used, and decide whether or not
they should remain on your list. Be aware that it is easier to add
something than it is to take it off the list. Over the years this can
make your load heavier and heavier. There is nothing wrong with
having something on the list that is seldom taken. This reminds
you to consider that item and then decide if it is appropriate for
the upcoming outing. If you don't want to take it, just check it off
without packing it.

I have included in this chapter reproductions of the lists I
used to prepare for my guided trips. They are customized for
canoe trips, but most of the items will be relevant to any activity
involving camping for an extended period. Use the lists, if you
wish, as a starting point in creating your own check list system.

Kitchen Pack: The major items in this pack, and the other
packs, will be discussed in more detail in the Camping chapter
starting on Page 33. I designed my kitchen pack so that wherever
I put it down I had a complete, self sufficient kitchen. Mostly, it
contains the tools needed for meal preparation, but some food
items - condiments, coffee, flour, etc. - are also included. Small
items are kept in plastic bags so they won't roll around loose,
cluttering things up. The equipment in the pack is of sufficient
size and quantity to handle up to 12 people, which was the maximum number I would take. The items on the list of contents could
be easily decreased if the party was smaller.

☐ Kitchen Boxes

☐ Pantry Box

- ☐ Cook set, cups, plates, etc
- ☐ Silverware
- ☐ Big spoon
- ☐ Spatula
- ☐ Grill
- ☐ Griddle
- ☐ Reflector oven
- ☐ Reflector oven pan
- ☐ Bread and cake pans
- ☐ Gas stove
- ☐ Water pails
- ☐ Coffee pot
- ☐ Leather gloves
- ☐ Water filter
- ☐ Extra matches
- ☐ Hand soap
- ☐ Paper towels
- ☐ Vegetable oil
- ☐ Coffee
- ☐ Coffee-mate
- ☐ Sugar
- ☐ Tea
- ☐ Clorox
- ☐ Sugar-cinnamon mix
- ☐ Pepper
- ☐ Salt
- ☐ Flour
- ☐ Jelly
- ☐ Pam
- ☐ Table Cloth
- ☐ Hand sanitizer
- ☐ Other _____

☐ Tool Box

- ☐ Folding saw
- ☐ Chain saw
- ☐ Gas & oil (chain saw)
- ☐ Axe
- ☐ Shovel
- ☐ Tarps (2)
- ☐ Ropes
- ☐ Toilet paper
- ☐ Dish pan
- ☐ Sponge
- ☐ Dish detergent
- ☐ Brillo
- ☐ Fly spray
- ☐ Medical kit
- ☐ Stove oven
- ☐ Canoe repair tape
- ☐ Extra plastic bags
- ☐ Fire pot
- ☐ Games
- ☐ Extra saw blades
- ☐ Extra tent pegs
- ☐ Tent plastic
- ☐ _____

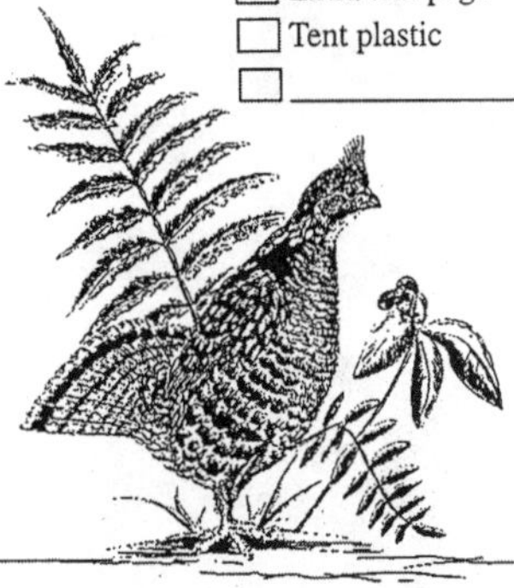

Photo 5 - The check list for the two kitchen boxes. We usually packed these for the next trip as we were cleaning up from the last one.

As an efficiency item, the pack itself was great - it saved me what would otherwise be endless rummaging for things ("Where is that spatula? I know I brought it), because all related items are in one place. The pack also provides a clean storage place for the kitchen items during the off season

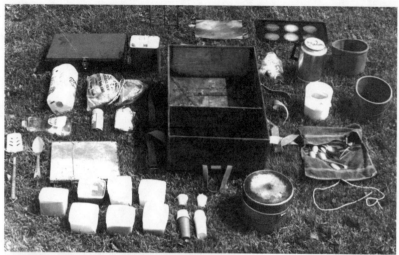

Photos 6, 7 - A kitchen box. Lower photo shows straps which allow the kitchen to be portaged by one person.

The pack I built for my own use is shown in Photos 6 and 7 along with what it usually contains. There is information on construction of packs in my book, *Building Outdoor Gear.*

Tool Pack: Your tool pack can be of about any design that appeals to you, but a design that allows you to access most items without undue pawing around will do wonders for your disposition when you want to find something in a hurry. I find that mine tends to be a catch-all that gets heavier and heavier if I am not diligent about removing unused items every so often.

Of course, there are items that you will want along and hope you never use, such as a first aid kit along with spare parts for tents, lanterns, stoves and anything else that might need emer-

☐ Food Packs

☐ Boxes
☐ Meals - menu
☐ Snacks - 1 per day
☐ Biscuit mix
☐ Bread mix (lunches)
☐ Extra coffee
☐ Extra sugar
☐ Extra paper towels
☐ Extra toilet paper
☐ Extra coffee lightener
☐ Extra stove fuel
☐ Other
☐
☐

☐ Cooler
☐ Ice
☐ Meals - menu

Items in ref & freezer:
☐ Cheese
☐ Onions
☐ Carrotts
☐ Apples
☐ Eggs
☐
☐

Photo 8 - **The food packs are packed in reverse order - last day on bottom, etc. The menu is used for the actual packing. This check list ensures the extras get packed.**

gency repair.

Food Packs: For the most part these packs are loaded by using the menu as a check list. When I returned from the market with the food I broke it down into breakfast, lunch and supper. Next, we did any prepackaging, cooking and other preparation

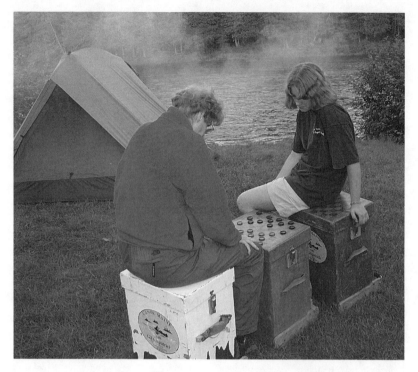

Photo 9 - **These are the food packs I used. The white one is a cooler that is lined with foam. Each are equipped with shoulder straps.**

that might be necessary. Now, with all the food out in plain sight (this is where I failed with the maple syrup) I packed the boxes with my menus as a guide, putting the last day's food in first and working toward the top. If the group was to be large, I used three boxes - one for each meal. Each food box was a different color, so I always knew which one contained each meal without opening them. I knew from experience that the breakfast box would have the most spare space, so I packed the extras on the bottom of it before I start packing the meals. The extras might be things like sugar, coffee, etc. With smaller groups the meals are doubled up into one or two boxes.

It is important to pack the food boxes as soon as possible after buying the food because everything is fresh in your mind and you know the quantities are correct, having checked them off the shopping list a little earlier.

Sometimes there is an extraordinary amount of bulky food. Usually in the beginning the food boxes will not accommodate this along with the other food. Just put the bulky items into a heavyweight trash bag and carry them that way for a day or so until there is some space in the food boxes.

Cooler: The cooler is actually one of the food boxes, but gets special consideration because it contains perishables. I tried several commercial coolers through the years and found most of them inadequate and some barely adequate. So, I built my own. I had two sizes, one for large groups and one for smaller ones. I packed the coolers using the same procedure as the food boxes - in reverse order from the menu. Once the cooler was packed I put the whole thing into a chest freezer and let the contents freeze. On the day I left for the trip I took the cooler out of the freezer. I then put perishables that could not be frozen on the top and I was ready to go. Packed this way I never had problems with spoiled food even during a week of hot weather. Any spare room I might have in the cooler I filled with plastic water bottles, frozen, which could later be used for drinking water.

For my large cooler, which took up way too much room in the freezer, I made an insert (box) of plywood in which I packed the food. The insert fit inside the cooler with some room for non-frozen perishables.

The beauty of this system is that by packing the unfrozen food and then freezing it, you have a solid block of frozen material with very little air space between the packages. This means it will hold the cold for a very long time. The only down side to this system is that you have to be aware that for the first half of the trip you will have to allow time for items to thaw.

On the bottom of my food pack lists I always listed perishables that could not be frozen. These were usually kept in the refrigerator until the morning of departure. This was to ensure that I didn't forget to pack them into the cooler before loading it into the truck.

The Guest's Equipment List: The following is extracted from my brochure, which each of my guests received before the start of a trip. Nearly all of my guests were not familiar with map and compass and so I did not require them nor did I furnish them. I did furnish whistles.

The following is a suggested equipment list. You may add to it if you wish, but bear in mind that you should keep your personal gear as compact as possible. **Most people take too much gear.** Everything on this list will go into or onto your pack bag, pack frame or duffel bag. A waterproof bag or pack for your gear is desirable, but not a necessity.

For summer trips (July and August):
1 pair shoes or boots for wet weather
1 pair of sneakers or moccasins
4 (or more) pair of socks (athletic sock weight)
4 (or more) sets underwear
2 long-sleeved shirts
2 long pants
1 lightweight windproof jacket
1 sweater or sweatshirt
1 rain suit or raincoat
1 hat with brim
1 set personal toilet articles, toothbrush, etc.
1 towel
1 swimming suit
2 bottles insect repellant
1 warm sleeping bag
1 foam or air mattress
2 large handkerchiefs
1 flashlight with extra batteries
1 cup, metal or plastic, with handle
1 bag or pack to hold the above
1 Pocket knife

Add the following to the above list for early and late season trips:
1 or more set of long underwear
1 pair warm waterproof boots
2 or more pairs of heavy socks
1 pair warm gloves or mittens
1 warm hat
1 winter jacket or coat

Optional Items:
Camera and film
Medicine as required
Spare eye glasses if needed
Snacks

Fishing gear
Sandals
Fishing license (mandatory if fishing gear is taken)
Shaving gear
Reading material
Belt
Shorts

Remember, you are going to live out of your pack for an extended period of time, so give some thought to packing so as to prevent daily unpacking and repacking. Use packages within your pack: Take appropriate size plastic bags and put related items together in them. The plastic packages slide in and out easily without disturbing the rest of the pack and the plastic helps keep things dry if the pack should get wet. Of course, items that are most often used should be near the opening where they can be readily reached.

For early and late trips, do not skimp on warm clothing. While it may happen that we have summer-like weather with temperatures in the 70's, it can just as easily be in the 30's and 40's with below freezing temperatures at night. Be sure your sleeping bag is warm enough. Summer rated bags will not do in the spring and fall in northern Maine.

The above list was what I considered the minimum for the kind of trip we were going to take. It was expected that each person would have their own idea of what was "necessary" besides the items that I listed. This is OK as long as the inexperienced person doesn't get too carried away like a family I had on a trip a few years ago.

It was a family of five with two children who were quite young. The other child was 11 or 12 years old. I guess the parents couldn't imagine the kids getting along without their entire inventory of toys. They had three very large trash bags full of them. The family had so much gear that other folks on the trip had to take part of it in their canoes. Unfortunately I did not realize the full extent of their gear until the trip was under way and then we were stuck with it. The youngsters hardly played with the toys and when they did it was only with the same one or two - obviously the favorites. After that trip it was my advice to families to take along only one or two favorite toys.

My Personal Pack: My list is just an extension of the one I

☐ **Personal Pack**

- ☐ Boots (Insulated for fall & spring)
- ☐ Moccasins
- ☐ Sandals
- ☐ Extra laces
- ☐ 4 socks
- ☐ 4 shorts
- ☐ 4 tee-shirts
- ☐ 2 long sleeved shirts
- ☐ 2 pants
- ☐ 1 jacket or sweater
- ☐ Heavy jacket (fall & spring)
- ☐ Gloves (fall & spring)
- ☐ Long underwear
- ☐ Belt
- ☐ 2 handkerchiefs
- ☐ Bathing suit
- ☐ Hat
- ☐ Rain coat
- ☐ Towel
- ☐ Washcloth
- ☐ Toothbrush
- ☐ Toothpaste
- ☐ Soap
- ☐ Razor and blades
- ☐ Shave cream
- ☐ Medical kit - small
- ☐ Sewing kit
- ☐ Spare stove generator
- ☐ Tools: (Scrdrvr, pliers, adj wrn, 7/16 wrn, plugs)
- ☐ Safety pins
- ☐ Pocket knife
- ☐ Emergency Pack:

- ☐ Fly dope
- ☐ Nylon rope
- ☐ Compass
- ☐ Maps
- ☐ Matches
- ☐ Lighter
- ☐ Flashlight
- ☐ Camera equipment
- ☐ Note book
- ☐ Plastic bags
- ☐ Sleeping bag and pillow
- ☐ Sleeping pad
- ☐ Emergency blanket
- ☐ Pack frame
- ☐ Canteen
- ☐ Extra batteries
- ☐ Cup
- ☐ Hunting knife
- ☐ Check book
- ☐ Cash
- ☐ Permits
- ☐ Glasses & case
- ☐ _____
- ☐ _____

Photo 10 - All items were not taken all of the time. This list, and the others, are designed to allow items to be considered each time.

gave to my guests. Most of the items that do not appear on their list are the ones that I used as a guide to do my job.

The small medical kit in my pack holds the supplies that are frequently used such as adhesive strips, antiseptic salve, aspirin, etc. My pack was always handy and so this saved digging out the big medical kit for minor scrapes and scratches.

☐ **Master List**

☐ Canoes
☐ Paddles - 3 per canoe
☐ Bailers - 1 per canoe
☐ Life jackets - 1 per person
☐ Tents
☐ Canoe poles
☐ Outboard motor
☐ Motor gas
☐ Motor bracket
☐ Canoe chairs
☐ Rescue line
☐ Cooler
☐ Kitchen pack
☐ Food packs
☐ Propane tank
☐ Tool pack
☐ Personal packs
☐ Tool box (truck)
☐ Spare trailor tire
☐ Sukey's bag
☐ Blue lunch bag: w/ spreaders, cutting board, plastic bag.
☐ Bag lunch and drink
☐ First supper
☐ Water Jugs
☐ Other: _____

Photo 11 - When everything was checked off on this list I was ready to go. Secure in the knowledge that nothing was forgotten.

I use two waterproof bags for my personal gear. The large one has shoulder straps. In it goes everything that I am not likely to need during the course of the day such as sleeping gear, extra clothing, etc. The other bag is small and also waterproof and holds items that I might want to get at while we are under way. It would hold such things as my raincoat, the small medical kit, map and compass, etc. I kept it within reach in the canoe.

The Master List: When all of the items were checked off on all the other lists, I was down to the master list. The main purpose of this list was to check the boxes and packs onto the truck and to remind me of the items that do not get packed into a container. This list was the last thing I looked at before driving out of the yard. On the bottom of this list I could also make notes of anything that I wanted to be sure to take care of before leaving home.

When my master list was completely checked off I left home with my mind clear to think about the trip ahead of us. I did not need to stop and think if I may have forgotten something. I didn't worry all the way to the river whether something I could not remember packing was there. *I knew! I knew* everything we would want or need was on the lists. *I knew* I checked everything on the lists into their containers. *I knew* I checked everything on the Master List onto the truck. It is a great feeling to start off with that kind of confidence!

Camping

The ability to establish and maintain an efficient, comfortable and environmentally acceptable campsite is a prerequisite to becoming a good outdoor leader. Your camp will define the kind of leader you are to even the inexperienced folks in your group. You don't have to know how to do something to recognize that someone else does, and knows how to do it well.

A place to camp has to be chosen and very often the leader has to consider several factors in making a decision. Once chosen, the camp should be set up quickly and efficiently and in accordance with rules and laws governing the area. People in the group should be given widest latitude possible in how they establish themselves in the camp, but the leader can save them a lot of grief by suggesting changes that might make them more comfortable.

For example, people often are attracted to a nice comfortable depression in the ground as a place to set up their tent. It has to be pointed out to them that they may wake up after a good rain thinking they are in a bathtub. Things like this are basic to taking care of people in the wilderness.

Choosing a Campsite:

The outdoor leader should be prepared for two different types of camping areas, ones that are established with at least some facilities such as a fireplace, and those that must be prepared from scratch. In some places the only legal campsites are the established variety. One would think, at first glance at least, that choosing one of these is a no-brainer, but perhaps not.

Established Campsites: On the Allagash Wilderness Waterway, where I did many of my canoe trips, it was legal to camp only in established sites. Still, it required some thought and experience to choose one of them to suit the conditions at any given time. I experienced several hurricanes through the years while I was on the Waterway. The first one was in the 1970's. I learned about it about eight hours before it was scheduled to hit our part of the state. My immediate problem was to get my party to the best possible campsite in which to weather the storm. With eight hours to work with I had 18 choices, a few more if I really wanted to push our paddling for the day. The dangers from a hurricane are the wind and the rain. I chose a campsite with high ground between us and the expected wind direction. It was on a side hill which ensured good drainage for the heavy rains that were sure to come. When we arrived I inspected the area carefully for trees and broken branches that might come crashing down during the storm (widow-makers). The slope, that attracted me to this spot with a hurricane eminent, is the very thing that made me avoid the site under normal conditions. There was no really good level place to set up tents.

The site turned out to be a good one. The wind was no problem for us and, while it was the heaviest rain I have ever camped in, the water ran off the side on the hill as fast as it fell. When I woke up in the morning it was pouring and the floor of my tent was rippling as it floated on the stream of water that flowed beneath it. I cannot say we comfortably weathered that storm, because it is impossible to stay dry in that kind of drenching downpour, but we were safe.

My hurricane experience is kind of extreme, but it points out that even among established sites there are choices to be made depending on the conditions at the time or expected in the near future. High winds may cause you to choose a site on a lee shore because it is no fun to set up tents, cook meals and go about other camp functions with things constantly blowing about. On the other hand if insects are a problem, or in very hot weather, it might be nice to choose a site that will take advantage of any breeze that might come along.

Whatever the agency responsible for establishing the site you choose, it will have rules for its use. Be sure you, as the leader, are aware of those rules and abide by them. If a fire is legal, there will be a fireplace and rules about cutting firewood. Most fire-wood regulations I have encountered allow cutting dead trees. Why anyone would want to cut, and try to burn, wood from live trees is a mystery to me, but some do.

All campsites should be left in as good, or better, condition than you found them. It is unpleasant, and sometimes infuriating, to have to pick up and carry out someone else's mess, but do it anyway. Sometimes the agency responsible for the site can only visit it one or two times through the season, so it is up to respon-sible campers to keep the place clean and picked-up. Also, many established campsites are there at the grace of the landowner. A garbage pile on the land may give the owner just cause to close the area to everyone.

From Scratch Campsites: Assuming it is legal for you to establish your own campsite, what should you look for? You may be surprised to find that, if the spot you pick has all the prerequi-sites of a good campsite, it very possibly has been used by some-one before. Many of the old established campsites have a long history of use. It is interesting that along their shorelines there can sometimes be found evidence of even earlier use - pre-his-torical use! I have frequently found chips of chert around old campsites where ancient First Americans worked at crafting stone tools centuries before. So, if you find evidence of previous occupation as you work at setting up your camp, you can give yourself a little pat on the back for seeing the same possibilities as others before you.

Your potential campsite should be above the flood plain so you don't have to pack up in the middle of the night and head for high ground when heavy rains cause the water level to rise rapidly. Many times these quick fluctuations in water level are the result of severe storms upstream that you may not even be aware of. This is an important point to keep in mind because flood plains often look like tempting places to set up camp. They are relatively flat and may be more free of brush and other material than other places.

You will need a level place for tents. The size of the flat spot will, of course, depend on the size of your tent(s). Usually it is OK to clear away some underbrush for a tent site, but avoid any heavy cutting unless you have landowner permission to do so. Tent sites should *not* be ditched. This was recommended practice years ago, but this environmentally damaging practice is a no-no for today's campers. Choose a site that will drain naturally and use tents with floors that will protect sleepers from getting wet from below.

Look for any potential dangers that might injure someone. If the area shows signs of heavy animal use, there is no reason to believe the animals will change their habits just because you choose to set up there. A moose stumbling through a tent in the middle of the night might make a funny story at some point in the future, if no one gets hurt, but it *could* cause serious injury to someone. Look around for widow-makers (leaning trees or large broken limbs that could come down). If you cannot take care of them, move on and find a more suitable spot.

If you plan to have a campfire you should ensure the area is suitable for it. You should be able to scrape away any forest duff and get down to mineral soil in the area around the spot you pick for the fire. Then a ring of rocks should be constructed to contain the fire. It is your responsibility to be sure that your fire cannot spread into the woods around you. Someone has usually taken care of this possibility in established campsites, but when you make your own, the responsibility is on your shoulders. It is an awesome responsibility when you think about it. You will also want to evaluate the availability of suitable firewood in the immediate area. This will probably not be the problem in a new site that it is in an old established one where the woods immediately around the area have been picked clean by previous campers.

Water is always a necessity that has to be considered. If you arrive there by water, that water is usually the source (We'll discuss making sure it is safe a little later on). You may want to look for a source that is clearer, colder, or closer to your kitchen area.

Finally, think about protection from the elements. Present or expected conditions should influence your decisions. Choose the spot that offers the most protection from conditions that present the greatest danger to your party for the time you will be there. It might be wind, rain, thunder storms, or even insects. In the late season be aware that heavy snows can collapse tents. Some overhead protection from evergreens will help prevent waking up under a pile of snow.

Shelters

Most everyone preparing for an extended outdoor expedition envisions it with bright sunny days with no rain, or if it rains, only at night. These ideal weather trips come along once in a while, but most of the time it just "ain't gonna' happen". As an outdoor leader you have to think about providing shelter to keep everyone as comfortable as is possible under outdoor living conditions. It always pays to buy quality when it comes to outdoor equipment and it is especially true when considering shelters. Don't skimp on equipment and be prepared for the worst, because if you do this thing long enough the worst will come along.

One of the things I managed to learn by looking around at other canoe guides and outfitters when I was getting started is that the tent of choice was the Eureka Timberline. So, that is what I bought. The tent comes in three sizes, 2-person, 4-person and 6 person. I chose the 4-person tent for two people to use.

Each size is available in the regular model and the Outfitters model. The Outfitters model is more than twice the price of the regular model, so I figured I could get by with the less expensive one. A mistake. It not only didn't last long under constant use, but we were forever making repairs. In a very few years I replaced with the Outfitters models.

Tents: Since I have already had my say regarding quality I will move on to other things. The style of your tent(s) will depend entirely on the type of outdoor activity you are planning on. If you are going to run a spike camp for hunting or fishing you may want to go with the big wall tents, perhaps one for sleeping and one for cooking and eating. If you plan on backpacking you will look for the lightest, most compact tent you can find and will probably want to forgo the luxury of putting two people in a 4-person tent as I did for canoe camping. There are plenty of different models out there to choose from.

The tent floors should be made of a material that is substantially heavier then the side walls (this was not the case with the regular grade Timberline). Even with heavy duty floors that are treated to be waterproof, you will find that water will find its way through pin-holes that develop over years of use. I always took along thin plastic (the kind you buy in a hardware store for a painting drop-cloth). This stuff takes up very little room in the tool box, and it can be passed out during periods of prolonged heavy rain so each guest can spread it over the inside of the tent to keep their sleeping gear and clothing off the damp tent floor.

Be sure to take along extra tent pins and any other parts of your tents that may be broken or lost. I usually came out even on tent pins. I always had spares in my tool box to pass out when needed, but we usually found about as many as we lost.

Tarpaulins: Even if you use the large multi-person tents it is nice to have a sheltered place outside. If your tents are small and meant mainly for sleeping, the covered area is a necessity. During hot summer months the tarps are as valuable for shade as for protection from rain. When it does rain you need a place, out of the rain, to prepare meals and for people to gather and eat. The

Photo 12 - **When it rains there is nothing like a good tarp for people to gather under. The boxes are used for tie-downs - they are built to be out in the rain, leaving room for people where it is dry.**

trials and tribulations of dealing with wet weather are bad enough with adequate shelter, but people's tempers are liable to get short if they have to stand around eating their meals in a downpour. Your own patience may suffer as well at having to prepare the meals under those conditions.

The most readily available tarps are the blue or green ones that are plastic and are nylon reinforced. They come in a wide variety of sizes and are equipped with an adequate number of grommets for tie-downs. The only fault I can find with this kind of tarp is that it is heavy and bulky. The tarps I used for canoe trips were made of nylon and were lightweight and compact. A 12 X 12 foot nylon tarp would roll up into a roll about 12 or 15 inches long and 4 or 5 inches in diameter. I carried two of them with me so I could cover an area 12 feet wide and nearly 24 feet long. This allowed me to cover the cooking/eating area as well as my fireplace where I did my baking. On rainy days the most popular place around is under the tarp, make it big enough.

Your tarp(s) should be permanently equipped with ropes so you can raise it quickly when needed. I found 1/8 inch braided nylon to be strong and easy to handle. I made each line 12 feet long which was adequate most of the time. But, I could tie on to it if a longer reach was needed.

Emergency Shelter: In an emergency situation where shelter from the elements is needed it is up to the leader to show some ingenuity. On a trip where we had to lay over because of weather, the wind was blowing hard directly into our camp. It was not only uncomfortable, but made it hard to get meals and keep the campfire going without using huge amounts of wood. We had the tarps up, but something else was needed. We brought up some of the canoes and leaned them against the pole that was holding up the tarp. Cozy.

In a survival type emergency a shelter can be made with natural materials at hand. I figured out as a young boy roaming the woods near home how to lay up poles against a tree and cover them with evergreen boughs. It is amazing how much water a shelter like that will shed. It is, after all, the same principle as a thatched roof which has been around for centuries.

If there ever is a time for the outdoor leader to show leadership, it is when shelter is badly needed. People tend to stand around and feel sorry for themselves in their misery. Put them to work helping to do whatever you determine the best course of action to be. It will get their mind off their problems and get the job done faster.

The Campfire

For a lot of outdoor people a campfire is a very important part of camping. It is expected. If you plan to use one for cooking then it is a must. Know and understand the rules governing open fires in the area you plan to be in. If a permit is needed, get it well ahead of time so you don't have yet another thing to deal with at the last minute. Before you leave it, your fire should be doused with water and stirred to ensure there are no live coals. It is a

***Photo 13* - A small camp saw will make short work of the wood cutting chore.**

good gesture to take out any unburned wood and pile it beside the fireplace so the next camper has a clean fireplace to start with. If you used the fire to burn some of your trash, check to make sure none of it remains unburned. If there is any, take it along with you.

Tools: Two tools are necessary to efficiently gather firewood. An ax (not a hatchet) and a camp saw. I have loaned my camp saw to countless campers over the years who thought only an ax would do to put up the firewood they needed. After watching my group quickly put up firewood for the evening and the following morning with my little bucksaws, they changed their mind. There are a variety of camp saws on the market or if you prefer to make your own there are plans in my book, *Building Outdoor Gear*. Be sure to take along a spare blade or two. If chainsaws are allowed where you are headed the little machine will make firewood preparation a very short and easy job. There are small ones on the market that are economical and are perfectly adequate for putting up campfire wood. A quart of mixed gas and a half pint of chain oil should do for a week. Don't forget to take along a file to touch up the chain in case you accidentally find a rock with it. And, take along a camp saw as well - machines *do* break down.

Finding Dry Wood: Campers have to be prepared to use what is available for firewood. As a boy I read the old camping books that advised: "...find a good supply of dry hard wood...." Well, lots of luck finding dry *hard* wood in my part of the country. The woods are predominantly fir and spruce and so that is what we use. I have cooked and worked over softwood fires so long I don't know if I could handle one made with hardwood. Adapt to what is available - pioneers on the prairie used buffalo chips!

Where campsites are used by many campers the area around the site will look to be bare of dry wood. However, most campers seem to have a certain distance beyond which they will not travel for firewood. I have always found plenty of good wood by going just a little further and finding standing dead trees for wood. Make sure the dead tree has been dead long enough to dry out. If there are dead needles on the branches, the tree is dead, but has not been that way long enough to dry out. Usually there will be some bark peeling off the tree if it is nice and dry. Fallen trees can also be a source of wood if they have not come into contact with the ground.

Another source of dry wood is to collect it while underway

providing your mode of travel will allow it. On rivers there are places where driftwood piles up along the shore and this can be a good source of dry wood. Just stop and cut it short enough to load into the canoe(s) and then finish cutting it up when you reach your campsite. Also the woods are full of standing dead trees where there are no campers to cut them. If you dislike walking so far around campsites for your wood, then stop at a likely spot along your route and spend a few minutes gathering firewood.

Standing dead trees are dry no matter what the weather. If you are setting up camp in a rainy spell a campfire will go a long ways in raising your spirits as well as that of your guests. Haul a dead tree into camp, cut it into foot-long pieces and then split out the dry wood inside with your ax. Split some of it up real fine for kindling and a few more pieces a little larger to get things going. After you have a good blaze you can use the rain-wet outer parts of the log as well.

Fire Starters: For a sure-fire fire starter I rely on birch bark. It works, wet or dry. Birch bark, like dry wood, is not to be found in the immediate area surrounding a well-used campsite. In fact, thoughtless campers destroy many birches around the campsites by cutting off bark with knives and axes. Don't do that. A supply of bark can be gathered during your days travel and stored in a small bag for future use. Any bark you can strip off the trees with your bare hands will not harm the tree in any way. The bark can also be found on the ground around birches where it has fallen off naturally. It is not a bad idea to carry along a few of the commercial fire starters that are available, or compact fire starters can be made by rolling pieces of newspaper and dipping them in wax.

Meal Preparation

As I explained in the Provisioning chapter, I never felt the need to demonstrate my culinary skills in the woods by whipping up meals from scratch on the spot. I knew I was capable of doing it if need be, but could never see a reason to do so with so many other things that need doing. Still, all meals do require a certain amount of preparation in the field, some more than others. My rule of thumb was that whatever I could do at home prior to the trip was time well spent. It is true that the kind of trip and the kind of food provided for the trip will have a large influence on the preparation. If it is an extended backpacking trip you will probably want lightweight dried food and will plan on cooking it on a one-burner stove. On the other end of the spectrum would be the permanent hunting camp where weight is not a serious problem and a multi-burner gas stove and/or a wood stove would be appropriate.

Campfire cooking: A lot of outdoor leaders have become a master of meal preparation over a campfire. I have watched them at work; they have made an art of it and can turn out a great meal without benefit of modern heat sources. Many established campsites have a permanent grates over the fire to make campfire cook-

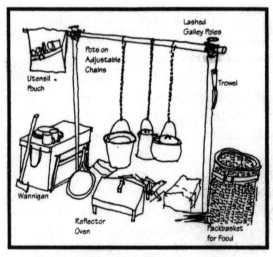

Photo 14 - **A detail drawing of the camp set-up shown in Photo 15.**

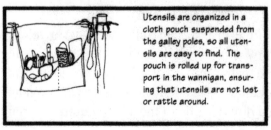

Utensils are organized in a cloth pouch suspended from the galley poles, so all utensils are easy to find. The pouch is rolled up for transport in the wannigan, ensuring that utensils are not lost or rattle around.

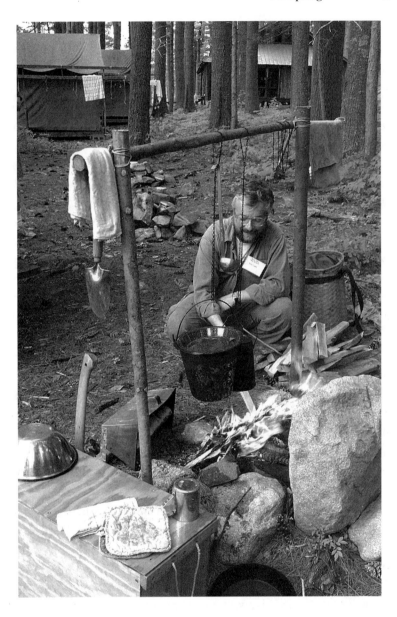

Photo 15 - This is Dave Lewis' camp set-up in a demonstration at the Maine Canoe Symposium. Notice the bread baking while the rest of the meal cooks suspended above the fire.

ing easier. The problem with those grates is that they are a constant distance above the fire. So, if the fire is a little too high
things overheat and if too low the cooking slows down accordingly. With the grate you must constantly try to adjust the fire to
meet the heat requirements of the moment. Not an easy thing to
do. A better way is to adjust the distance of the cooking pots
from the fire.

The best system I have seen for campfire cooking is demonstrated by Maine Guide, David Lewis in Photos 14 and 15. The
two poles are driven into the ground on each side of the fireplace.
A crosspiece is tied in place from which the pots will be suspended. The old-time books have pictures showing a forked stick
to hold the crosspiece, but that is seldom practical. Try driving a
forked stick into the ground without breaking or splitting the fork.
Lightweight chains are used from which to suspend the pots. The
chains have "S"-hooks attached to them so adjustment up and
down is quick and easy. You want to just keep something warm -
pull it up high. Boil some water in a hurry - lower the pot down
close to the flames. What could be simpler or easier to do?

Another distinct advantage of the chain system over the grate
is that a reflector oven can be used at the same time the rest of the
meal is being prepared in the suspended pots. Very often, if a
grate is lowered over the fire, it prevents the oven from receiving
the even heat it would get from an unobstructed flame.

Most everyone who has tried campfire cooking knows about
one serious drawback. The cooking utensils are going to get black.
If that is a problem for you then you should probably look for an
alternate method, because it requires a lot of scrubbing every meal
to remove the soot. The answer to this problem is to let the kettles
stay black and manage your packing system to accommodate
blackened pots in such a way as to not contaminate the rest of the
items in the box or container.

If campfire cooking appeals to you it will allow you to travel
a little lighter - no stove and fuel to lug around. It pays to remember though, you will be dependent on a wood supply and on your
ability to build and maintain a cooking fire no matter what the

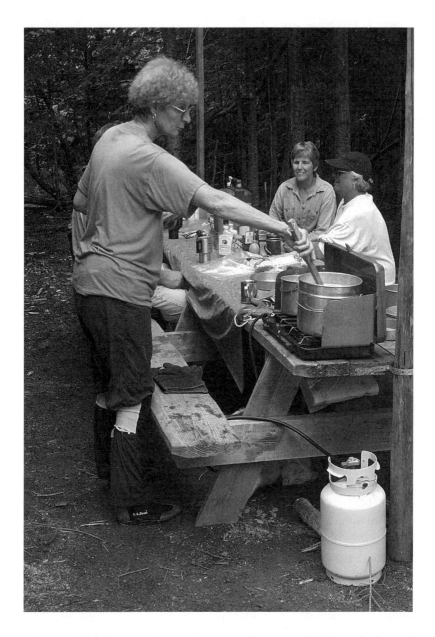

Photo 16 - **This is a propane stove converted to use refillable tanks instead of the disposables. The tank shown is 11 pounds - just about right for a week of camping with a large group.**

weather. You should definitely have a tarp along to cover the cooking area when it is raining. No matter how good a fire builder you are, a good downpour will put it out leaving you with no way to cook the meal.

Camp Stoves: Camping stoves vary in size from those little one burner jobs, favored by backpackers, to the large two and three burner stoves for folks who don't carry everything on their back. There are some exceptions, I guess, but most of the camp stoves use either gasoline or propane for fuel. They are both dependable and clean to use.

For many years I used the gasoline stoves for my canoe trips. I was satisfied with them even though I had to replace them every four or five years because the sheet metal they were made from would rust through. Since I gave them more use in those few years than the average camper would in a lifetime I accepted this as normal. Around 1990 my new stove would not adjust correctly. It would flame out when I tried to adjust it to a low heat or it would blow back into the mixing chamber. It was frustrating and I thought I must have gotten a lemon. Rather than complain I replaced it with a new one. Same problem! I decided it was time for a change.

I bought a propane camp stove. Most propane stoves are set up to burn propane from small disposable tanks. I was not interested in using the disposables because of the expense and the inconvenience of having to carry along several of them, full and then empty. An inexpensive kit allows conversion from the disposable tank set-up to that of using a refillable propane tank. The usual 20 pound tanks are larger than needed for most trips, but smaller ones are available. Having no experience to call upon, I had trouble deciding whether to get the 5 pound or the 11 pound. I played it safe and went with the larger of the two. It was a good choice; I seldom used over 5 pounds on a week-long trip, but once in a while I did. For emergency I carried along one of the disposable tanks. I was glad I did.

While unloading, at the shore where we were going to start a four day canoe trip, I smelled propane. I guess I was too numb to realize it might be my own, so I continued unloading until I came to my tank. Somehow the jostling around in the truck had opened the valve enough to release the gas. As it turned out I had enough left to last three days and needed to break out the emergency supply for the fourth. After that trip I drilled a hole in the valve handle so I could wire it in the closed position when transporting.

All in all I would rate propane above gasoline for camp cooking. I was glad I changed. It is easier to get going (no pumping) and the cooking heat more readily adjusted. You do need a little wind protection, but you do with gasoline too. The propane tank is an extra item to pack along, but it requires no more space than a gallon or two of gasoline.

My cooking method for camping used both the propane stove and the campfire. The most of the meal was prepared on the stove while the biscuits or bread was baking by the campfire.

Reflector Oven Baking: If you have camped for more than a day or two you know the problems involved with providing bread for your meals. It goes stale in a couple of days and usually it gets flattened so a loaf resembles one big slice. There is a way around this problem and it can be a lot of fun as well. Bake your bread every day! Nearly every evening meal I prepared was served with hot fresh baked biscuits. They were served with the breakfast as well except on pancake days. I baked a loaf of Canoe Country Bread every evening for the following day's lunch. I usually had it ready to go in as soon as the supper biscuits came out so it could be baking while we ate supper.

Generally speaking, there are two methods of baking in the out-of-doors. One is the Dutch oven. This is a large covered kettle made of cast iron or aluminum. For baking, coals are placed under it and in its cover and the items to be baked are placed inside. It has two disadvantages for the camper. It is heavy to lug around and it requires long lasting coals which require a dry hardwood fuel source - hard to find in some areas.

The most practical baker for the outdoor leader is the reflector oven. It has been around for many years. Cooks for river driv-

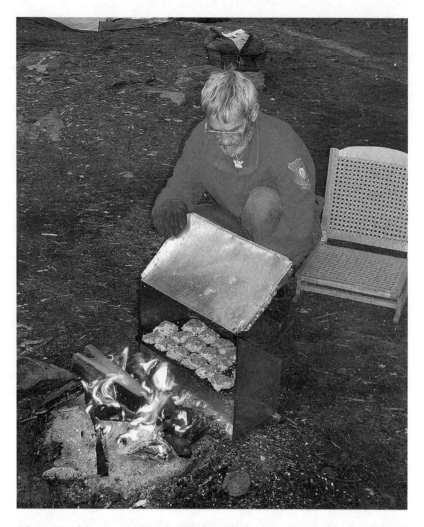

Photo 17 - **Most guests are very pleasantly surprised to be served fresh baked goods on a week-long trip into the woods. It isn't hard to do and will make you a hero every day.**

ers in Maine used them to feed their hungry crews. They set up four of them around a fire in order to provide biscuits and bread to fill the ravenous crews at the end of a cold, wet day on the river. Reflector ovens rely on a blazing fire rather than hot coals. This means dry wood, split into small pieces, is the best fuel.

Reflector baking is easy. Anyone can do it with a little attention to some basic rules that will ensure success. A reflector oven is needed, obviously. To bake for up to six people an oven that is about 12 inches wide will do just fine. If you plan to bake for larger parties an oven 18 inches, or more, wide is recommended.

Choose dry standing fir, spruce or cedar for your fire wood. If dry hard wood is available it will do as well. Cut it to about 12 inches and split it small enough to create a blazing fire. A fire that has been burning for a while will ensure a hot base and will contribute to creating a hot blaze when the dry wood is added. Place the oven in front of the fire and watch the biscuits or bread closely for a while. If it is too close to the fire the front edge of the bread will start to burn. If this happens back the oven off a little. After a few tries you will develop an instinct for the correct placement of the oven. Even with careful watching it isn't unusual to have a little charring on the edges, but if that happens just remember what my mother used to tell me when she burned the toast. "It makes you a good singer!"

You will have to turn the bread at least once and probably more as the side closest to the blaze will cook faster then the rest. At times the items will be baked but will lack that nice golden brown crust that we all like to see. If this happens just pull the oven a little farther away from the flame and allow a little more time. This can also be done to keep the baked goods hot while you finish up the rest of the meal.

It is an easy matter to carry along the makings for fresh baked goods. Bisquick can be turned into biscuit dough by the simple addition of water. Add enough to make a stiff dough and then drop spoonfuls onto the baking sheet. Almost any quick bread can be done with a reflector. I use a home made mix I call Canoe Country Bread which we serve daily on canoe trips. The recipe is on Page 59. You are not limited to baking bread either. We always carried along a cake mix on our trips in case someone was celebrating a birthday while we were out. Brownie and cookie mixes are available and are easy to use, and you can use your own recipes as well.

As I pointed out in the Provisioning chapter, we always premeasured and packaged our mixes before leaving home. This allowed us to just take out a package, add the water and mix - no measuring required on the trail. For Bisquick, four cups will make 24 biscuits, so for smaller groups two cups for 12 biscuits would be sufficient.

Camp Kitchen Hygiene: The need for cleanliness doesn't stop when you leave home. It is easy to forget when living outdoors where the normal rules and mores of living are a little more relaxed. Because of this the outdoor leader has to be vigilant about his own habits as well as those of anyone who may be assisting. Before any meal preparation is started, the hands should be thoroughly washed. Besides being the thing to do, even if you were there all alone, it shows your guests that you are concerned about their health and well-being. Hand washing is not as convenient in the field as at home so we used the waterless hand cleaners that are on the market today. They don't excuse the initial hand washing for the start of the meal, but in the outdoors we handle a lot of unclean things as we work in meal preparation. A squirt of the hand cleaner does the job for in-between times. It seems to have alcohol in it so it evaporates in a few seconds and you can go back to work. A small bottle of the stuff takes up little space in the camp kitchen box.

Clean-Up: Dish washing is an important part of the business of feeding a group of people in camp. Rubbing the dish with a little sand down by the riverside may be good for the movies, but it just doesn't cut it for real life. Most of us today realize that, just as clear water isn't necessarily safe water, a clean looking dish is not necessarily a safe dish. The outdoor leaders job is to ensure everyone in his or her care has a good time. Sick people do not have a good time.

Dishes should be washed as soon as the meal is over with hot water and then dipped in a rinse of boiling hot water (water that has boiled). We always used a pliers-like gripper for the hot water dip. Take along some tool that will allow you to do this. Some campers recommend using gloves for the dish washing so that the wash water can be boiling hot as well. I'm not sure this is necessary as long as you use wash water as hot as your hands can

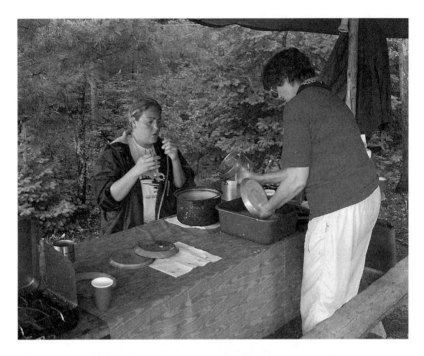

Photo 18 - **Dish washing. Hot soapy water for the wash, boiling hot water for the rinse. The rinser is using grippers (pliars would work) to dip the dishes into the hot water.**

stand it, and then do the boiling-hot dip. Biodegradable soaps are available for dish washing, but ordinary detergents are probably OK as long as you dispose of the dish water at least 300 feet from the nearest water and in dense vegetation where it will be absorbed.

The hot dip rinse usually eliminates the need for wiping your dishes unless you want to pack them away immediately, and even then the hot dishes dry so quickly that little wiping is needed. Even if you do all your cooking over a gas stove, it is a good idea to have a large pot available to keep hot water going over the campfire. Mine is always referred to as the "black pot" for obvious reasons. This is not only a ready source of hot water for clean-up, but is there for the guests to help themselves if they want a cup of tea or whatever. Be sure the water has boiled at least five minutes before use unless you are sure it comes from a safe source.

Safe Water: It would seem that if the water where you are has not flowed by any human habitation that it would pure and OK to use. However, there are a variety of organisms that occur naturally in free flowing waters no matter how remote the area may be. The best known of these dirty little germs is giardia which causes what is commonly known as *beaver fever.*

Ever since I was a little boy I have roamed the woods and have drank water from brooks, streams, lakes, rivers and even woodland pools. Because of this I assumed I was immune to anything a wilderness water could throw my way. I was wrong! After I returned home from a week-long trip I came down with giardia,. Without going into detail I will just say that I will take every precaution in the future to prevent getting it again.

Even springs should be suspect. It is certainly possible for organisms to be in spring water so you will have to be the judge and take your chances if you use the water untreated. Remember, you are risking the health of others.

The easiest and most common method of treating water these days is with one of the filter pumps that are available from outdoor outfitters. With one of these you can safely filter and drink water from just about any source. Of course, the cleaner the water is to start with, the longer your filter will be effective. Use the clearest source of water available.

I have been carrying and using one of the filters for years, but I also used the simple method of treating water with chlorine. Carry along a supply of Clorox® in a dropper bottle of some sort and you have an almost instant method of making water safe. Two drops per quart of water will be sufficient for relatively clear water. If the water is a little murky use four drops per quart. The effect of this treatment is said to be practically instantaneous, but we try to do it at least 10 or 15 minutes before the water is to be used. There will be a slight chlorine smell, like many municipal water supplies, if the treatment is sufficient. We usually use this treatment when the water is for something other than drinking. This saves a lot of pumping yet safe water is ensured. We use the filter pump for drinking, thus avoiding the city-water taste. Iodine tablets are also available for water treatment.

Five minutes of boiling is another method of making water safe. Cooking water is treated this way as it does its work, and you will boil water for dish washing.

It is a good idea to carry along a container of water for party use between campsites. Water bottles and canteens can be re-filled from it during the course of the day. Replenish the container each evening with water treated with whatever method you are using. We used two 2-1/2 gallon plastic containers for this purpose, these were easier to handle than one 5 gallon one.

Dealing with Waste: A lot has changed since I first went camping with my father in the 1940's. Most of the food people took to the woods back then was in cans. No one even considered carrying the empty cans back home. The accepted practice was to burn them in the campfire and then bury them. The fire destroyed the protective finish so they would rust away quickly. If you camped in an established, well used, campsite it would have a dump somewhere nearby where solid waste could be deposited. Sometimes the dump had a crib made of logs to contain the waste. Of course, garbage also found its way to those dumps, and no one thought of cleaning the cans before throwing them out, so animals were attracted to the dumps. The cans, jars and bottles were often scattered far and wide. Many of the old dumps have been cleaned up by volunteers and the long-used campsites now show no sign of the former litter.

Carry in, carry out is the slogan most campers are familiar with today. It makes so much sense that it is hard to understand why it used to be otherwise. After all, if you can carry a *full* can into the woods, how much trouble is it to carry an empty one out? Still, we should not judge our forefathers by today's standards. I always tried to limit my cans and bottles to the barest minimum to avoid having to carry around the empties. When I did have them I washed the empties along with the dishes so they could be stored in any available storage box without contaminating it. The empty can takes no more space than it did full.

If you keep a campfire you can dispose of paper goods by

burning them and so cut down on your load of trash. It isn't a good idea to burn plastics. Wash them out and carry them along with you.

Uneaten food presents a problem especially on trips of a week of more. It is bound to get real ripe if you carry it along for that long. Some folks disagree with me, but I successfully dispose of most garbage by burning. Let me hurry to explain that I do this only when I have a very hot fire and plan to maintain it for an extended period of time. I defy anyone to find traces of garbage in my fireplace when I break camp. The only alternative to burning is to have a container with a very tight seal in which store garbage. Even then the animals that find the smell of rotting food attractive will find it. Burying is not an environmentally acceptable solution, especially in the area around campsites. I see nothing wrong with burying in a remote area (a mile or more from the nearest campsite). It will be found by animals there, but so what? It isn't as if you are establishing a dump where animals will visit habitually.

The way you handle human waste will probably be influenced by the length of your stay at the selected spot. If it is just an overnight thing the best way might be to instruct your guests to dig a six inch hole (cat hole) and each bury their own. If your stay will be for several days it is best to dig a latrine about two feet deep and have everyone use the same spot. A log fastened between two trees will make the thing a little more comfortable and if you really want to go first class you could take along a toilet seat to set up over the trench. Instruct your guests to push in a little loose soil each time the latrine is used. In any event be sure you take along a small shovel with which to do the digging.

Some people are very thoughtless when it comes to their own waste. Campsite outhouses are not the sweetest smelling places to spend your time and folks accustomed to the sterile bathroom with a flush toilet will sometimes rebel at entering one. I have found piles of human feces and toilet paper right in the path to the outhouse, left there by gross, thoughtless people with sensitive noses. If there is no outhouse at your camp be sure to impress on everyone in your group that whenever they leave the area with a roll of toilet paper in one hand, they better have a shovel in the other. Draw your own conclusions from the following story involving my dog, a Border Collie named Sukey.

At the conclusion of every meal Sukey insists it is time for her and I to take a walk. She insists on it! We were camped at the junction of the St. John and Big Black rivers. About five or six hundred yards upstream on the Big Black there is a bridge. Someone has cut a nice trail along the river between the campsite and the bridge - a pleasant place to take Sukey for her mandatory walk. At two different places along that beautiful trail were deposits of human feces, right in the trail, with the tell-tale pieces of white paper in case there was any doubt of the source. As we continued our walk toward the bridge I noticed Sukey leave the trail. I watched and saw that she was squatting and leaving *her* deposit about 10 or 15 yards off the trail in the woods. 'Nuff said?

Extra-Curricular Activities: There are bound to be times on any extended trip into the woods when there are periods of inactivity - most often brought on by the weather. To prepare for those times I always tried to provide at least a few activities for folks to while away the time. On the covers of my food boxes I painted a checker board, and always had a sack of checkers in the tool box. The board would also accommodate chess, but I found it difficult to keep a full set of chess pieces. A deck or two of cards is also a good idea. On one trip a cribbage board was fashioned from a piece of driftwood. This not only provided a game for them to play, but must have occupied the craftsman a long time in the making.

Very often my guests would come up with some unusual, on-the-spot games that were good for a laugh. One of the funniest of these was a sport called "Crotch Rock". To compete, the player squatted about half way down over a fair size rock with the arms *behind* his/her legs. The rock was then picked up from that position and thrown forward. Sounds easy? Try it!

I always took along reading material for myself and encouraged guests to do it as well. Many times you can include books about the area you are visiting, they will be of immediate interest to people in your group. If space permits you could also take along guides for trees, wild flowers, animal sign, birds, etc.

The outdoor leader is responsible for ensuring the camp is legal, environmentally acceptable and safe. Establish your camp rules with these things in mind early on and enforce them. Diplomacy is the watchword when it comes to enforcement, especially if you are being paid for your services. A short explanation for your "requests" is always better than trying to "order" someone around.

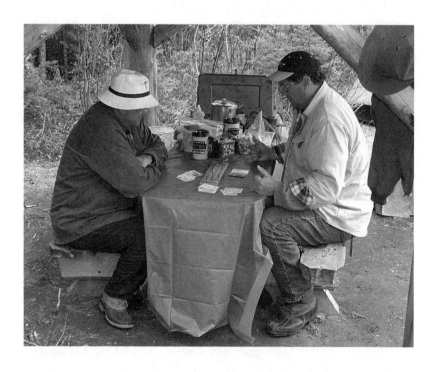

Photo 19 - On this trip cribbage was the game of choice.

For the Camp Cook
Recipes and Ideas

There are several books written about camp cooking and they include many recipes and ideas for turning out appetizing and nutritious meals in the out-of-doors. I have read some of them and have picked up an idea or two from them. Mostly though, I have done my own thing and tried out ideas as they came to me. Some of them worked out, some were abandoned after the first try. Not being a purist in any sense of the word, I have no qualms about doing things the easy way. If there is a prepared mix available from the super market that I like, I use it. New mixes are always coming along so keep your eyes open, as you prowl the super market isles, for something new to try out.

The Provisioning chapter with the menu and shopping lists give a pretty good idea of my choices for a menu and the food to fill it. There are some things that have worked out so well, and have been so popular with my guests, that I have included this short chapter to pass them along.

Canoe Country Bread: Browsing through a 100 year old camping book one day, I came across a recipe for bread. That's what it was called, "bread". I gave it a try and it turned out to be the best bread I have found for day in, day out use on any outdoor expedition. It can be baked in a reflector oven, stove-top oven or what have you. One loaf takes care of six people for lunch with cheese, peanut butter, etc. Dry ingredients are taken pre-mixed. All I do is add the water, mix and bake.

4 cups flour
4 teaspoons baking powder
3 teaspoons salt
1/2 cup sugar
2 1/2 cups water

The mixed dry ingredients are taken in a plastic bag. To use, put the dry mix into a bowl or pot, add the water and beat the devil out of the batter for a half minute or so. Pour the batter into a greased or oiled 7 X 11 inch pan, or equivalent, and bake for 45 minutes to an hour. In actual use on the trail, the time or temperature means little. A stick should come out clean, then it is done. The shallow, 7 X 11 inch pan is used rather than a loaf pan to cut down on the baking time. Also, it is more versatile than the loaf pan, lending itself to other uses.

All kinds of variations are possible. Try adding dry fruit like raisins, then streak in some cinnamon-sugar mix and you have a tasty coffee cake.

The bread was without a name in the old book, so I took the liberty of naming it. I think it is just about the same as bannock bread that was an old-time camping staple. Bannock was often baked in a skillet propped up in front of a fire; no doubt this bread could be as well.

Allagash Muffins: I wondered what I would do if I had no oven, but had Canoe Country Bread mix on hand. I tried this and it worked out fine:

4 cups of Canoe Country Bread mix
1/4 cup of flour

Carefully add water to the bread mix until you have a stiff dough. Using flour to keep from sticking, make patties of the dough about the size of English muffins and about 1/2 inch thick, a little thicker is OK. If you don't have extra flour along just save a little of the bread mix aside (before adding the water), and use that.

The muffins can be cooked on a griddle, skillet, grill or anything else you can get hot. They are probably the best cooked on a forked stick over the hot coals of a campfire. Eat them hot with butter, jelly, sugar-cinnamon mix, or whatever appeals or is on hand.

Camp Biscuits: All you need for these is a biscuit mix. I use Bisquick, but you can make up your own if you like. Four cups of the mix will yield 24 biscuits. Carry along pre-measured dry ingredients according to your needs for each meal.

No need for a rolling pin for these. Add the water until you have a fairly stiff dough. Not real stiff, but not runny. Drop the dough by the spoonful on a baking sheet and bake in the reflector. Drop biscuits are a lot easier to make than the roll-out variety and they taste just as good.

Biscuit mix has many uses in camp, so look through the recipes and also use your imagination. Take along a little more than you think is necessary in case a new opportunity comes along. Also, extra biscuits will stretch a meal if need be.

Maine Guide Breakfast Buns: These buns go great with any breakfast where bread is called for. The recipe given makes 24 buns, but can be easily reduced or increased. I often use leftover buns for lunch to stretch the Canoe Country Bread.

4 cups Biscuit mix (Bisquick)
2 or 3 tablespoons of cooking oil
2 eggs
Sugar-cinnamon mix
1/2 box raisins

Stir in the wet ingredients along with the raisins and enough water to bring the dough to a thick consistency. When well mixed, drop by the spoonful on a baking sheet and then sprinkle the sugar-cinnamon mix on top of each. Bake in a reflector oven until golden brown.

Any of the above ingredients can be omitted (except the biscuit mix) without seriously effecting the outcome. Other available ingredients could be substituted; you can use up whatever is on hand, including fresh fruit. Not having any spare eggs in no excuse, make it without them.

Hot Chocolate Mix: If you want to make your own instead of buying a prepared mix:

1 cup unsweetened cocoa
1 cup sugar
4 cups powdered milk
1/4 teaspoon salt
Use 1 1/2 cup of mix to 1 quart of water.

Stuffing Mixes: These are delicious, and filling, additions to most any meal. Use them when you feel the need to stretch out your other items, like when there is an unexpected mouth or two to feed.

They are lightweight to carry and easy to prepare. Available in a variety of flavors, they can be made and set aside to free up burner space for other things.

Some Fixin's for Chowder: It is a good idea to have your menu pretty well planned out in advance of any outing. However sometimes things come up that require a change. It is a good idea to try and expect the unexpected. I came across this item while guiding a canoe trip. The time of the year was not good for fishing so I did not take fresh potatoes or other vegetables for a fish chowder, not expecting anyone be fishing. One person did though, and he caught a beautiful 24 inch togue (lake trout).

A chowder was in order so I dug into the food pack to see what I could find. The only thing to spare was a couple of packages of scalloped potato mix and some corn and onions. That was it! It made a great fish chowder. The cream mix for the scalloped potatoes was a substitute for the milk (along with some dried milk that could be borrowed from a breakfast meal) and the rest of the items just fell into place.

The boxes of scalloped potato mix take up little space and can be used to add to any other meal if not used for a chowder. Repackage to take even less space.

Macaroni & Cheese: This is a meal that is near universally popular, yet is inexpensive and easy to carry and prepare. Of course you can buy the boxed mac & cheese meals from the super market shelves and make it even easier to carry and prepare, but I think you will find this one a little more satisfying.

I usually serve this meal on the last evening out because the ingredients keep well so there is never a chance of spoilage. I received a real compliment from a guest who was on his second trip with me. As we sat down for the last evening meal of macaroni and cheese, he apparently had forgotten that it came last when he remarked, "I was afraid we weren't going to have my favorite meal this time".

The recipe is to serve 12 people.

9 cups of elbow macaroni
1 1/2 to 2 pounds of sharp cheddar cheese
1 can of evaporated milk
2 tablespoons of oleo
2 tablespoons of flour
1/2 teaspoon of salt
1/4 teaspoon of pepper
1/4 cup of finely chopped onion

Cook the macaroni in a gallon or more of boiling water. Drain when done.

To make the cheese sauce: Combine the milk, oleo, salt, pepper, and chopped onion in a pan and heat over low heat so as not to burn the milk. Cut the cheese into small pieces and combine into the heated mixture. Stir often to melt the cheese and prevent sticking. Just before you are ready to stir the cheese sauce into the macaroni add the flour to the mix to thicken it a little. Stir into the macaroni and serve immediately with green peas and biscuits.

Penobscot Cobbler: Here's where you can really impress your companions on any outing. This is one of those places where some extra biscuit mix comes in handy. When fresh berries are in season you can do something a little more creative than just sit down and eat them off the bush.

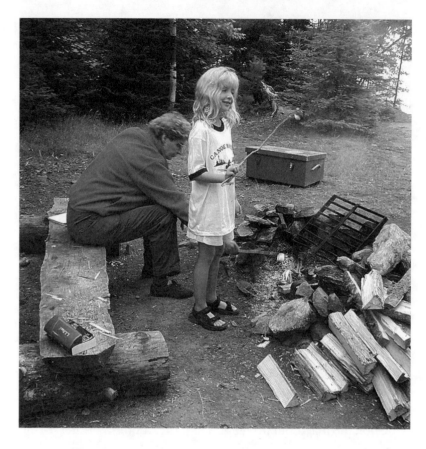

Photo 20 - **Roasting Marshmallows. Some things are better if cooked by the eater!**

    4 cups of fruit or berries (any kind)
    2 cups of biscuit mix
    2 or 3 tablespoons of oleo (if available) or oil.
    Seasoning (Pre-mix at home for just such an occasion)
        1 1/2 cups of sugar
        2 tablespoons of cornstarch
        1/2 teaspoon of cinnamon
        1/4 teaspoon of nutmeg
    If no berries are in season and you still want to make a cobbler you can take along a dried fruit which can be re-hydrated.
    Gently stir the berries and the seasoning mix together in a

large pan. I use the frying pan from my cook set.

Add a dollop of oleo to the biscuit mix and add just enough water to make a stiff dough. Spread and flatten the dough with your hands or a make-shift roller until it is the shape of the pan and a couple of inches larger in diameter. Place the flattened dough over the berries and tuck in the edges and seal them to the edge of the pan with your fingers like a pie crust.

Bake in a reflector for about 30 minutes. Usually when the crust is browned the cobbler is ready. Cool before serving.
***

Maine Guide, David Lewis along with his wife Lynne and daughter Samantha share the following favorite recipes:

Dave and Lynne's Dried Fruit Cobbler: Mix or pack at home:

Topping:
   1/4 cup brown sugar
   1/2 cup flour
   1 cup dried fruit
   1/2 teaspoon baking powder
   1/4 teaspoon salt
Filling (pack separately):
   1 cup mixed dried fruit
   1/2 cup sugar
   1 teaspoon cinnamon

Trail Directions: Mix filling mixture and 1 1/2 cups of water. Simmer until tender. Place in a deep, greased and floured pan. Cream 3 tablespoons of butter and add the pre-mixed ingredients. Mix all together and sprinkle over the cobbler filling.

Bake for about 30 minutes or when a wood sliver inserted in cobbler comes out dry. Turn the pan about half way through.

Samantha's Brownies: Mix or pack at home:
6 Tablespoons of cocoa
1 cup sugar
1/4 teaspoon salt
1/2 cup flour
3 Tablespoons powdered whole egg

1/2 cup nuts, raisins or gorp

Trail Directions: Melt 6 tablespoons of butter. Add: 1 teaspoon vanilla, 6 tablespoons water and pre-mix ingredients.

Mix all together. Bake in greased and floured pan such as a small chafing dish insert. About 6 inches square by about 2 inches deep. The brownies are done when a sliver of wood inserted into the middle comes out dry, about 30 minutes, turning the pan every 10 or 15 minutes.

Dave and Lynne's Bread or Rolls: Mix or pack at home:

2 cups flour

1/2 cup white wheat flour

1/2 cup bread flour

2 teaspoons sugar

2 teaspoons instant yeast

1 teaspoon salt

Trail directions: Mix together with 1 cup (-ish) warm water, adding extra flour or water to make a firm, almost sticky dough. Knead for about 10 minutes, and let rise in the bowl. Punch dough down, shape into a free-form loaf or individual rolls and let rise on the reflector oven pan, either covered and placed in the sun, or near the fire (not too close). Bake. Bread is done when it sounds hollow when thumped. The bread is enough for two meals, a dinner and some lunchtime sandwiches, for two adults and a toddler.

Canoes *and* *Canoeing*

The canoe is the most versatile watercraft ever invented. Its longevity alone makes that point. The birch canoe predates the white man in America by several thousand years - it was here and widely used when the first Europeans stepped ashore. Early manuscripts tell us how impressed the newcomers were with the boats used by the natives. Ancient canoes were of two major types, the bark canoe (birch being the best known), and dugouts. I am sure the dugout preceded the birch canoe, but it must have been heavy and would not have allowed the freedom of movement that was achieved with the lightweight birch bark canoes.

It is safe to say that the birch bark canoe has been around for five thousand years or more. I once made the statement, in an article I was writing about canoes, that the birch bark canoe could have been invented right in my home state of Maine. I received a call from the editor asking me for the source of this information. I replied that I couldn't find information to the contrary. He ran it as I wrote it. Of course no one knows, so if you live in an area where canoe birch (white birch) grows you can make the same claim without fear of contradiction.

Champlain was the first European to use native canoes as he searched for the legendary Northwest Passage through North America to the Orient. He nearly drowned in La Chine Rapids (China Rapids) on the St. Lawrence. He named the rapids as he was sure he had at last discovered the elusive water route.

In his book, *Penobscot Man*, Frank Speck made this statement about birch canoes, "[The birch canoe]...is the most complex and intricate product of native mechanical genius in the north." It has always seemed ironic to me that the two major inventions of the Native Americans, the canoe and the snowshoe, were quickly adapted by the white man and allowed him to travel, settle and wrest the land away from people who invented them.

Outdoorsmen today use the canoe in a wide variety of outdoor activities; fishing, hunting, wilderness travel, racing, and recreational canoeing are some of them. The overall shape of canoes has not changed all that much over the millennia, in spite of modern manufacturer's claims to the contrary. What has changed in the last 50 to 60 years is the materials they are made of. This change to tougher, more resilient materials has changed the way people use and treat canoes. The birch canoe and the wood canvas canoe were somewhat fragile and didn't stand much rough treatment without the need for immediate repairs. The tougher canoes started with the aluminum ones built right after World War II by aircraft manufacturers looking to make use of machines and workers when the demand for war planes disappeared.

Many of the modern canoes are made with plastics that are tough and durable. This in turn has developed a canoeing style that is often oblivious to rocks and other obstacles that were carefully, and skillfully, avoided by the old-time canoeists. Still, it is important to learn the canoe handling skills that allowed the old-timer to keep his canoe afloat. The outdoor leader who uses canoes for his or her outdoor activity should pay close attention to the correct handling of the craft in all kinds of water conditions.

The Canoe

It would be necessary to have several canoes to have the correct size and shape for every purpose. People who are really into canoeing do just that, but most people are content with one or two and so a compromise is necessary. The size and shape you choose will depend on how you intend to use it the most. If you are going to use it mainly for a cargo canoe on lakes then a large canoe with a keel would be called for. However if you are going to use it mainly to run white water rivers then you will probably choose a canoe without a keel and with some rocker. If you plan to use a motor on it all the time then a square-stern model might be practical.

Size: In my years of using and building canoes I noticed that nearly everyone who was interested in getting started with canoes chose one too small for what they had in mind. The only reason for this that I could come up with was that they were more familiar with boats. They knew that a 15 or 16 foot boat was a pretty good size, so determined the same must be true for canoes. It isn't. A canoe 16 feet long is adequate for a couple of people to go fishing or canoeing with little or no extra gear. A canoe for canoe camping trips or for use where heavy loads are expected, should be at least 17 or 18 feet long and most guides in Maine prefer 20 footers.

All dimensions of a canoe can vary - width, depth and length, but the most significant variant is the length. Think of it this way. Compare an 18 foot canoe with a 20 footer. Where is the extra two feet in the longer canoe? Right in the middle! Right where the canoe is the widest and so where the most floatation will be achieved. The ends of the two canoes are essentially the same.

The example above makes it clear that even a six inch increase in length can make a significant difference in the amount of weight the canoe can safely carry. The usual rule of thumb for safe loading is to be sure you have at least six inches of freeboard. This means the gunwales of the loaded canoe should be six inches above the waterline. However, common sense has to be used in loading a canoe as with anything else. If waves are

2

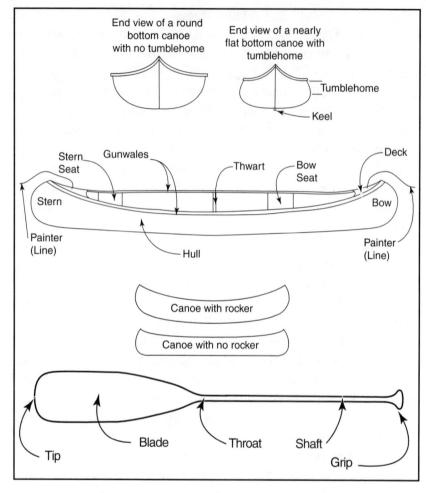

Figure 1 - **Canoe and paddle parts and some canoe nomenclature**

high on a lake or the loaded canoe must be taken through rough white water, then a lighter load, thus more freeboard, would be called for.

Shape: For a work canoe I prefer a canoe that is wide, quite deep with little or no rocker and is 20 feet long. My work canoe had no keel and the bottom was slightly rounded. The sides were not flared, but had no tumblehome either. This canoe is, of course, a compromise because my canoe trips were for the most part equally split between lakes and rivers. If necessary I could load this canoe with a half ton of people and gear and still have six inches or more of freeboard.

If I was going to limit my canoeing to either lakes or rivers I would choose a more specialized canoe that was more suited to the conditions. A canoe with rocker has a definite advantage in white water. It is quick to respond to paddle strokes and so will turn quickly - a real advantage when running through rock strewn rapids. For strict lake paddling a straighter bottomed canoe would be in order and the overall shape would be like the work canoe I described above. Many people would prefer a canoe used in lakes to have a keel. I feel that a keel is superfluous on a canoe and limits its versatility. Once you become used to controlling a clean-bottomed canoe you don't need any help from a keel.

If the canoe is to be used with a motor most of the time you might want to consider a square stern model. This makes the canoe rather specialized and, while it can be used without the motor, it lacks the handling characteristics and classic beauty of the traditional canoe shape. A side mount works well on larger canoes and, though they look to be out of balance, work very well. You can mount up to a six horsepower outboard on a 20 foot canoe. Then you load the canoe, and shift your own weight to balance the canoe and keep it on an even keel. The mount and motor can be quickly removed and the canoe reverts back to the classic form. A canoe that was especially designed for motor use is the Grand Laker. It was designed, and first built, in the Grand Lake area of Maine.

A final thought on choosing a canoe for your particular activity is this. Look at what others in the same activity are using. If they have been at it a while, they know what works best.

Material: The outdoorsman today has a wide selection of materials when choosing a canoe. A lot depends on what he or she plans to do with the canoe and how much time is available for maintenance. It also has a lot to do with his or her personal likes and dislikes - you have to be happy with your equipment to enjoy using it.

In my own case, with a book out on building strip canoes, I

would never let myself be seen in a canoe of any other type of construction. I did, however, provide canoes for my guests that were made of materials a little more forgiving of the mistakes that novice paddlers were likely to make. A couple in Maine have a guiding service that uses only locally built wood-canvas canoes and they pack their gear in pack baskets of the type used in Maine in the nineteenth and first part of the twentieth century. They like the "traditional" equipment and their success proves that their guests do too.

The following discussion of canoe materials is by no means a complete listing of what may be available. If you are interested in making your own canoe by any construction method in common use, you already know the limitations of the canoe without me telling you. Decide what fits your needs and then look at what the dealers have to offer.

Aluminum was the first of the indestructible (almost) canoes. It was the most commonly used canoe by guides and outfitters from the end of World War II until the early 1970's. Its major advantages were its toughness and the fact that it was maintenance free. It did have some disadvantages that made it objectionable to serious canoeists and other outdoors people. It was noisy - a serious disadvantage to hunters and fishermen. The noisy canoes were also embarrassing to canoeists who inadvertently hit a rock - the bass drum-like sound announced that fact far and wide. The metal canoes had to have a keel because of the way they were constructed. Efforts were made to minimize the keel, but it still had to be there so the two sides of the canoe could be riveted together. In white water the aluminum would stick to rocks that canoes of other materials would slide over easily. A disadvantage of much concern to serious canoeists was the fact that the method of forming aluminum limited the shape of the resulting canoes. It was even more limited than the older canoes made with wood and a *lot* more limited than the various plastics that came along a little later.

The first of the plastics were commonly called fiberglass canoes. They were made in a negative mold using woven fiberglass material and/or fiberglass mat as reinforcement and then the material was wet out with a resin. The advantage of molded canoes was immediately apparent to serious canoeists. Now it was possible to make a canoe of virtually *any* shape. Later another reinforcing material came along which made possible a lighter, and even tougher, canoe - Kevlar. Kevlar is a very strong material while being extremely lightweight. Kevler is the material that bullet proof vests are made of. For canoe construction it is wet out with resin as with fiberglass, but has the disadvantage that it is not transparent when finished. For this reason it is shunned by strip canoe builders and others who want the wood to show through. I do find a use for it on my working strip canoe, however. I put a football shaped piece of Kevlar on the bottom where it doesn't show when in the water. It stands up beautifully to the day to day banging around in white water, and dragging up on rocky shores, that a working canoe has to withstand.

A little later other plastics came along which were maintenance free and even more forgiving of mistakes than the fiberglass canoes. One of the first of these was commonly called Royalex. It remains the most durable and most used by outfitters and guides who require a long lasting canoe that is as near to indestructible as possible. The material is correctly called acrylonitrile-butadiene-styrene. No wonder everyone knows it as simply, ABS. I have had guests wrap an ABS canoe almost completely around a rock with no more damage than a slight wrinkle in the surface and perhaps a kink in the gunwale. The canoe was straightened out on shore, and with no further repairs needed, was used to complete the trip.

The only disadvantage to ABS is the expense. They are more expensive than most of the other plastic canoes. In order to appeal to a wider market canoe manufacturers needed a moderately priced plastic canoe. Polyethylene was the material that filled the bill. It is tough and inexpensive. Though the material is inexpensive, the molding process is not. Because of this it is the material is found in mass produced canoes made by large companies like Coleman and Old Town. Large numbers must be produced in order to justify the cost of the molds.

This is admittedly an incomplete discussion of canoe sizes, shapes and materials, but is meant only to give an outdoor leader a place to start. If you are looking to buy a canoe or canoes for any outdoor activity, I think it is important that you satisfy yourself and have what feels good and that you enjoy using. I know I feel a sense of satisfaction every time I paddle a strip canoe I have built myself. I am sure my friends who use "traditional" wood-canvas canoes have a similar feeling. Even if there is disagreement about materials, the advocates of one may still agree with another about size or shape. Satisfaction, like beauty, is in the eye of the beholder. If you need a canoe that you can bang around and never have to maintain, then there is satisfaction in having a canoe that will take it.

On the Water

If you are leading people on an outdoor expedition involving canoes, whether for hunting, fishing, exploring or just for the sake of canoeing, you need to prepare them for it and prepare yourself to take care of them. A lot of people have paddled a canoe. That doesn't necessarily mean they know much about canoeing, although many will answer that they are experienced if asked. Observe them carefully and then determine the level of instruction that is needed and the kind of canoeing you feel secure in allowing them to undertake. It often requires a great deal of diplomacy to deal with people who think they know more about canoeing than they can demonstrate. Take it slow and introduce new methods in a way that will help them and not injure their ego or pride.

Personal Floatation Devices - (PFD's): On a number of occasions I have been on a large lake when a sudden , unexpected wind came up - not an uncommon occurrence in mid-summer. When this happens I always think to myself, *what a blessing these things are*. They are a blessing especially to one who has the responsibility for the lives of others. The margin of safety these PFD's give when one is unexpectedly dunked is unbelievable

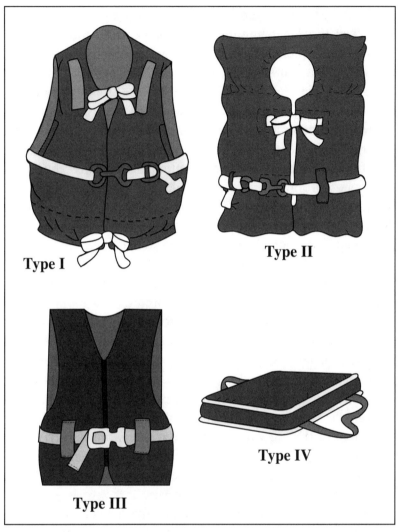

Figure 2 - **The four main Personal Floatation Devices. The Type I is orange with reflective strips. The Type II is usually orange. The Types III and IV can be any color**

unless it has been experienced. The colder the water, the greater the benefit, and the greater the believer in life preservers you become.

PFD's are made in five types and numbered with Roman numerals. These classifications are in the order of decreasing usefulness or desirability. That is, if you found yourself struggling in cold water, you would be far happier to be wearing a Type I PFD than to be hanging on to a Type IV. Only the first three should be considered suitable for canoeing. PFD Types I through IV are illustrated in Figure 2 along with information about each. Type V includes devices such as water ski belts and are not suitable for canoeing nor are they legal in most places.

Most outdoor people use either the Type II or III PFD's for general use. They offer good protection and, if good quality items are chosen initially, will last a long time. The Type III PFD's are the more comfortable of the two although they may be warm during hot summer months. During colder times of the year they do offer some protection from the cold and this can be especially important if someone ends up in the cold water.

Be sure to know and understand the laws regarding PFD's in your state. Also, be aware that the laws may be different for children than for adults. In Maine, where I live, there must be a wearable (Type I, II, or III) for each person in the boat, but the law does not require they be worn. For children age 10 and under, however, the law requires they be worn at all times while on the water. Regardless of the law, you should ensure there is a wearable PFD for each person and that it is of the proper size for the person who will wear it.

When PFD's are worn, be sure they are worn properly with all zippers zipped and all fastenings fastened. The life jacket does little good to the person in the water if it comes off and floats away because it was not worn properly.

No item of equipment is more important for your guest's well-being and safety than their life preservers. You can have a lot of things go wrong on a trip and still rate it as a success, but if there is a death or serious injury that you could have prevented, *man, you're a failure!*

Paddling Instruction: On my guided canoe trips I frequently had people with very little canoeing experience and with no formal instruction. Sometimes there were folks who had never been in canoe before! Because of this inexperience it was necessary for me to teach paddling techniques for both flat water travel and

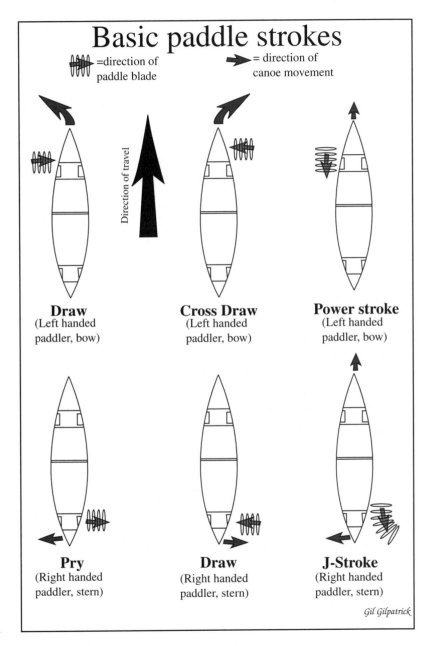

Figure 3 - The basic paddle strokes needed to successfully negotiate white water. Once mastered, they make flat water paddling a lot easier as well.

for managing their canoe in white water, which would be coming up in only a very few days. The instruction had to be as simple as possible and yet develop enough skill to negotiate Class II-plus rapids.

You will find, as I did, that just because you know the strokes and have used them for years, doesn't mean you know how to teach them. I was surprised how incompetent I was at teaching paddling skills that I knew so well until I did a little studying and learning of vocabulary. You gotta' know how to talk the talk before you can teach them to walk the walk.

I found that it was necessary for novices to learn only three basic strokes each for the bow and the stern paddlers. There are many, many named canoe strokes, but early on it became apparent to me that they all are simply combinations and variations of these basic strokes. The system worked well for me and with a few hours of practice, on quiet water, nearly all of my guests made a successful white water run. The basic strokes are illustrated in Figure 3 on page 77.

The outdoor leader should have people practice the basic strokes on flat water with the bow and stern paddler working together to control the canoe. Look at Figure 3 and imagine the two canoes on the left of the page are one, with a bow and stern paddler. The bow paddler does a draw and the stern paddler does a pry. The canoe moves sideways to the left, just as one would want it to do in whitewater to avoid a rock or whatever. Likewise combine the two center canoes in Figure 3 and the results of the strokes will move the canoe sideways to the right. You will have to demonstrate the cross draw and insist that they practice because it feels strange and unnatural at first. Point out that the two strokes illustrated in the two center canoes, the cross draw and the pry, are the most powerful ones they will have at their disposal.

The two right hand canoes in Figure 3 show the simple power stroke for the bow and the J-stroke for the stern. Novice paddlers have a tendency to hold their paddle at nearly a 45 degree angle while making a power stroke. This results in more of a sweep

Photo 21 - The girl in the bow is swinging over to do a cross-draw. She looks like she has done it for years, but in fact this is her first whitewater run and she has only had a few hours instruction while on flat water. Instruction and practice pay off!

than a power stroke, and makes the canoe harder to hold on course. Show them how to hold the paddle shaft nearly vertical while making their stroke. Also point out that the lower arm, holding the throat of the paddle, should be straight, not bent, as they pull the paddle through the water. That way the large back muscles do most of the work instead of the arm muscles.

The J-stroke takes a little getting used to, but make them practice it until it comes naturally. It is the most efficient means of keeping the canoe on course. Show them that the thumb of the hand on the grip points sideways through the power part of the stroke and then is turned downward as the paddle makes the J-turn. If it points upward, they are doing it backwards - ruddering. Point out that the J-stroke is nothing more than a power stroke with kind of a pry at the end of it.

I never tried to introduce any other strokes. I found that if they became even marginally competent with the ones illustrated in Figure 3 that they could handle the canoe nicely in white water. I had them do the following exercises in preparation for their white water run.

With little or no forward motion of the canoe, I had them move the canoe to the left (left hand canoes, Figure 3) and then to the right (center canoes, Figure 3). Once they mastered that maneuver I would have them spin the canoe on its own axis by doing the opposite strokes. This technique taught them how to turn the canoe to point upstream in a current - a safe way to go ashore. These three maneuvers are all they need to successfully avoid obstacles and to get their canoe safely ashore if necessary.

Reading, and Running White Water: Here again keep it simple. It takes a lifetime of experience to read whitewater well, but you can give them a little information that will give them a start in the right direction. The outdoor leader who is taking beginners should be wary of whitewater more difficult than Class II. Class III and above should be portaged, at least at first, to allow the novice paddlers to get the feel of moving water and how it effects their canoes.

Point out the V's that are found in white water and show them examples. By looking at the examples they quickly grasp that they must avoid the V's that are pointing upstream (usually caused by rocks), and head for the ones that point downstream. No further instruction is necessary to get them started, but they will begin to pick up the finer points on their own as the trip wears on. Encourage them to look at disturbances in the water as they pass them so as to determine what caused them. This will speed up their ability to read the water.

It is a good idea to talk over the whitewater each day and listen to what they say about it. At first they will try to avoid every standing wave, mistaking it for a rock, but in time, and with your assurance, they will learn to distinguish between the two. If there is time, and your guests are eager and able students of whitewater, you can start teaching other whitewater techniques. Things like eddys and eddy turns, ferrying and setting.

Photo 22 - **Lining a canoe through a difficult spot. This can save a lot of loading and unloading. The person in the rear does most of the work, while the person in front helps keep the canoe in line with the current.**

If you have several canoes in your group you should establish the order of procession. If there is an experienced person with you in another canoe, designate that canoe as sweep (last). Make yourself first and then establish the others with the following rules:

1. The lead canoe is never passed.
2. The sweep never passes any other canoe.
3. Each canoe keeps the canoe behind it in sight, waiting if necessary.

Lining: It is frequently possible to let loaded canoes down through an unrunnable stretch of whitewater with the painters. When this is possible a great deal of time can be saved because a portage is avoided. The leader should give instruction and then observe his/her guests closely because it is very possible to upset a canoe with the line. Instruct them to keep the pressure on the stern (upstream end) while using the bow line only for steering. A lateral pull on the either line can upset the canoe. Tell them that, like running whitewater, the important thing is to keep the canoe running parallel with the current.

Most canoes come with a hole for the painter at the highest point in the bow and stern. A line attached in this way may lead to an upset while lining because any lateral pull will be from the top and could cause the canoe to capsize. Many experienced canoeists make an attachment at or near the waterline to avoid this problem. This is easily done by drilling a hole at the desired point and installing a short piece of pipe with epoxy. Another, in the field, remedy is to make a yoke of rope attached to seats or to thwarts. The yoke (rope) goes around under the canoe and the line is attached to it under the canoe, in the center, so that any pull is from the bottom.

Poling: There will be times that an outdoor leader will find it necessary to get her or his canoe upstream. The fastest and most efficient way to do this is by poling. You as a leader should at

Photo 23 - A pole can be a great help in working a canoe upstream. The bow paddler can help with the steering. (Notice the little guy peeking around the box!)

least be familiar with the basics.

A canoe loaded for poling is heavy on the downstream end. This holds true whether going upstream against the current or downstream with it. If you were in an empty canoe going upstream a position just behind the center thwart would be about right. For downstream work just forward of the center thwart would be correct. In a loaded canoe or with a passenger, you would have to adjust your position accordingly. Anything will do for a pole, but if you really get into poling you will probably want to get one of aluminum, about 12 feet long. Hardwood poles work well, but are heavier. A pole can be made from a young spruce tree of suitable diameter. Work the large end down to suit yourself.

Practice on a shallow lake shore. Stand with your feet as far apart as possible and at about a 45 degree angle to the centerline of the canoe. Face whichever direction is comfortable for you. Start off by just pushing off with the pole and get the feel of it. You will find that you will have to correct, or steer, just as you do when paddling from the stern. A little pull before you lift the pole from the water will do the trick. Make thrusts with the pole and get the feel of it and of the steering technique. Later on you will want to try the "climbing-the-pole" method. This is helpful in going against the current. It is simply hand-over-hand until the top of the pole is reached. Then quickly reposition the pole and do it again.

When you feel comfortable poling in flat water, find a slow moving stream and give it a try against the current and then with it. Snubbing your canoe downstream in rapids is also a useful skill at times. It allows you to stop and pick your way through the rock gardens. Old time guides would never think of going downstream through rapids with a paddle.

If you have a bow person in your canoe you can save a lot of energy when poling upstream by having them do the steering. They simply draw left or right while you provide the power with your pole to buck the current.

Whitewater Upsets: Before setting off with your guests on

Photo 24 - **This is a classic broached canoe. The two canoeists are in position to lift the canoe free (which they did).**

their first white water run it is important to brief them on the potential dangers. Here you must walk a fine line. You don't want to scare them to death, yet you must impress upon them that there is an element of danger involved.

Start by telling them that it is important to keep their canoe as near to parallel with the current as possible. If they see they cannot avoid hitting a rock, it is better to hit it head on, than to attempt to avoid it and broach on it. Most times the head-on hit will cause the canoe to slide off to one side or the other or, if the rock is just below the surface, the canoe may slide right over it. However, accidents happen to all of us, so they have to know what to do if they see they are going to bump a rock broadside. Tell them to *lean downstream*, or into the rock. Explain that, though it is an unnatural reaction to lean toward something you are going to hit, it is important to prevent that upstream gunwale from dipping below the water surface. By leaning downstream they are exposing the rounded bottom of the canoe to the rushing water, which will flow harmlessly beneath it. If kept upright, most likely the canoe will either slide off the rock and continue downstream or will stabilize there so the paddlers can safely deal with the situation.

The novice paddlers must be told how to deal with finding themselves upset in whitewater. A pre-briefing. Tell them not to panic. I had a couple of youngsters upset once and they screamed all the way through the couple of hundred yards of current. They were not hurt and the water was relatively warm. If I had been in Florida instead of Maine I would have sworn they were in the jaws of an alligator. They just screamed for the attention. Tell them if they follow your instructions the worst that will happen is they will get wet.

The first, and most important thing for them to remember, is to ensure that they do not get downstream of their water-filled canoe. It will weigh over a ton filled with water and to get pinned between it and a rock could be fatal. Once they make sure that they and their partner are clear of the canoe they should face downstream, raise their feet to near the surface to ward off obstacles. Then, with an easy, simple backstroke, they just allow the current to carry them to a quiet place where they can be helped and help themselves. Assure them that their personal floatation device (PFD) will keep them afloat and that they will be safe in that position. If they can help steer the awash canoe through the rapids *without endangering themselves*, it might prevent damage to the canoe. They can do this by remaining at the upstream end and working to keep it aligned with the current. If possible they should hang on to their paddle. Warn them not to try to stand up in fast current, it could result in getting a foot caught on bottom and the rushing water can hold them under. They would almost surely drown before help could reach them.

Though it may seem a minor thing, the vocabulary used by tandem paddlers can be important in the noise and excitement of a whitewater run. Verbalize the commands they should use between each other so there is no misunderstanding. Two personal incidents brought this home to me. My wife, Dot and I were taking our first day trip of the season with our two daughters. We pushed off into a fairly heavy current and before we could get the canoe under control it was apparent that we were going to broadside on a fallen tree (strainer). Instead of yelling "lean downstream" I shouted, "don't lean upstream." All they heard was "lean upstream", and over we went. The second incident was with my mother in the bow. We lined up on a safe looking V in the water ahead and my mother held her paddle expectantly, waiting for a command from me. I said, "its all right". She thought she heard "draw right", and she did. In this case I was able to overcome her draw and we made it through OK, but a stronger paddler could have pulled us into a rock. I learned to choose my words more carefully.

If members of the party are downstream of an upset they should be instructed to watch for items that may come floating down and also to stand by to help when the people in the water arrive. If they are upstream of the upset, warn them not to endanger themselves by trying to help while negotiating the whitewater themselves unless they can go ashore to do so.

Rescues and Recoveries in Whitewater: No matter how good your instructions there will be canoe upsets from time to time. Most often these are no more than an inconvenience which require no special skills to get the people, canoes and gear out of the water. Many of them occur as a result of inattention in rather slow moving water that is easily waded. However, from time to time there will be upsets that will challenge the leader's skills, resourcefulness and leadership. These are the times a leader must prepare for.

There are a couple of good books on the subject of whitewater rescue that cover the subject much more thoroughly, and in more detail, than is possible here. The one I have read is *River Rescue* by Les Bechdel and Slim Ray. Another, that was recommended is *Whitewater Rescue Manual* by Wayne A. Sundmacher. Both can be ordered from amazon.com or most bookstores will order the books for you if not in stock.

The leader's job, first and foremost, is to look after the people. The equipment and gear are always secondary. So, when an upset occurs look immediately to what needs to be done for the people concerned. Every situation will be different and so you will have a different solution.

A frequent situation after a canoe upset in white water is to have people stranded on a rock in the middle of the river. You may be able to throw a rescue line to them and assist them ashore with it. Tell them to keep their feet near the surface and allow the current to swing them ashore. If the water is extremely cold they may be very reluctant to get back into it. In that case you must find a way to get them off in a canoe. If they are on a rock then there will be an eddy behind it. Get your canoe to the eddy by ferrying out from shore or by going upstream and doing an eddy-turn behind the rock. Talk calmly to the stranded individuals so they don't get excited and upset your canoe in their eagerness to get off the rock. Once you have the wet canoeists ashore you should take time to make sure they are comfortable. Get them into dry clothing. Build a fire if necessary. Once everyone is secure and comfortable, you can worry about recovering the canoe and any other gear.

In any type of rescue or recovery look for, and try, the simplest, easiest and fastest solution first. One of my guests broached a canoe on a rock in swift current. The occupants of the canoe were able to get ashore with no problems, but as I looked at the broached canoe I visualized an all day job of ropes and levers and systems of mechanical advantage. I knew that the rest of the day spent here probably meant spending the night in the immediate area as well. So, added to the problem of recovering the canoe was that of finding a suitable camp site and setting it up. Though I had my doubts as to the possibility of a simple solution, I decided to try. Two of us got into the water upstream of the canoe. We reached down and lifted from the bottom. Off it came! I was so surprised that the canoe almost got away from us as it floated free. I was able to lunge for the painter and managed to guide the canoe through the rapids and eventually to shore. The simple solution took less than an hour rather than all day!

If you are anticipating serious white water you should have at least 100 feet of rope, at least two carabiners and/or pulleys as well as extra pieces of rope to allow you to set up some kind of pull to recover a broached canoe. Nylon rope should be avoided as it has so much stretch that you will use up all the take up travel stretching the line leaving none to move the canoe. Some whitewater enthusiasts take along a hand winch or come-along. Most of these are capable of a 12 foot, one ton straight pull or a 6 foot pull of two tons. They are very useful when needed but are extra weight and bulk the rest of the time.

There are some useful principles and methods that will often help in freeing a broached canoe. (1) Rolling the canoe a quarter

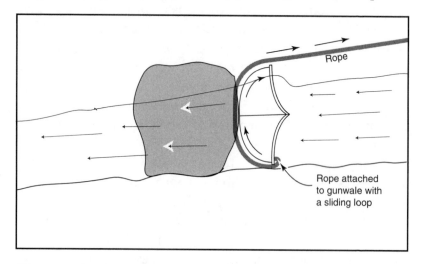

Figure 4 - **This is the way to roll a canoe to relieve the pressure of the water. Sometimes called the Steve Thomas rope trick.**

turn will present only one side to the current instead of the entire top. (2) Most times the canoe's position will favor swinging one end or the other downstream. Work this to your advantage. (3) If you are going to use mechanical advantage (Z-drag, hand winch, etc.) do not attach your line directly to painters, thwarts or seats. They will be torn out. Attach to the entire hull (See Figure 4). (4) Sometimes heavy poles can be used to apply leverage to the hull to raise or turn one end. To use this method the current must be such that a person or persons can safely stand up in it to apply the leverage of the poles to the hull.

Before setting up a recovery from shore, be sure to try the simplest methods first. If you cannot move the canoe by hand (the very simplest), you will have to attach a rope as illustrated in Figure 4. The line should lead over the high side of the canoe, and be fastened to the thwart. To do this, first tie a loop (bowline knot is recommended) around the thwart. Next run the line around the end of the canoe so it goes around the hull. Now by pulling

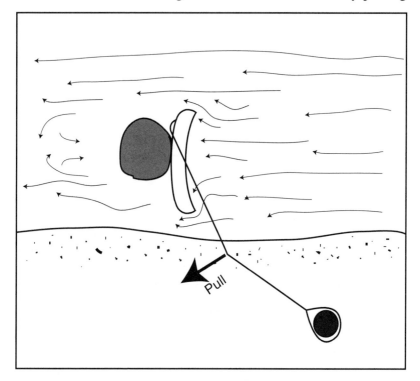

Figure 5 - **The vector pull**

up on the rope the loop will slide to the end of the thwart that is under water. Once the rope is in place the next simplest thing is to try to roll the canoe by pulling up on the rope while standing on the rock. Failing this you have to move on to more complicated and time consuming methods.

The time consumed in recovering a canoe that requires ropes from canoe to shore can be considerable. In my own part of the country it is complicated by the fact that most rivers and streams are bordered by 10 or 15 yards of dense alders before there are

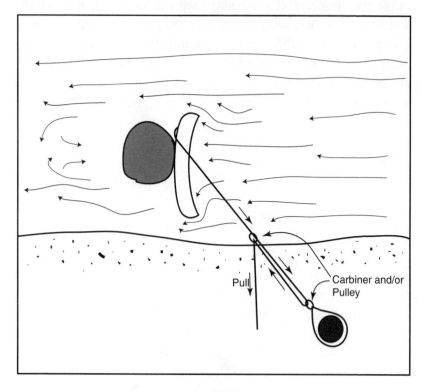

Figure 6- **The Z-drag set up.**

Photo 25 - Steps in tying the Prusik. The first step is sometimes called a larks-head knot. The Prusik is completed by just going around two more times. A tightened Prusik is shown on the right. The Prusik is easily moved back and forth on the rope allowing quick adjustment as the pull line is taken up.

Photo 26 - **An actual Z-drag set up. The black arrows show the direction the rope is moving as pull is applied to the rope on the far right.**

any trees that are of sufficient size to apply the pressure necessary to move a broached canoe. I imagine that in some parts of the country there could be a problem finding a tree. Period. Canoe recovery requires ingenuity!

The next easiest solution is the vector pull (See Figure 5). The line is attached to the canoe as shown in Figure 4. Next the line is taken from the canoe to the shore and secured to a tree or other solid object. The angle of pull has to be determined by the leader. Once the line is attached on shore and secured as tight as possible, the line is pulled laterally by as many people as are available. The people doing the pulling should be as near to the center of the rope as is possible under the circumstances.

The last resort solution is to use a Z-drag or the hand winch. If the winch is used, only a straight pull from a handy tree is necessary as the mechanical advantage of the winch supplies the needed power. Set up the Z-drag as illustrated in Figure 6 and

Photo 26. The use of pulleys in combination with the carabiners will reduce friction. The carabiners allow the quick attachment of pulleys where needed and makes them easy to move as the recovery proceeds.

Remember to have some way of controlling the canoe when it comes free of the rock. Usually this involves having a line attached to the painter that will be upstream when the canoe breaks free. With that line the awash canoe can be guided through the rapids to quieter water. What you want to avoid is getting the canoe broached on another rock, perhaps more seriously next time!

Nearly every rescue and recovery in whitewater will cause the outdoor leader to use all of the common sense and ingenuity he or she can muster, because seldom are two situations the same. Remember to worry first about the people. The canoe and equipment can be replaced, they cannot!

Repairs to canoes are sometimes necessary. The outdoor leader should always have a supply of duct tape on hand for this purpose. It will serve to cover holes in the hull, but can also be used to repair and replace broken thwarts, seats and gunwales. There are any number of other uses for duct tape on a canoe-camping tip, so take plenty.

Rescues and Recoveries in Flat Water: The classic method for the recovery of an overturned canoe in flat water is the canoe over canoe method as shown in Photo 27. The photo shows the recovery being demonstrated in very calm water, but in fact the outdoor leader must realize that it is seldom necessary to do this unless there are waves and winds present that contributed to the canoe upset in the first place.

The first thing to consider is the welfare of the people in the water. Hopefully they are wearing PFDs, but if not get them into them as soon as possible. As you approach the people in the water talk to them to determine their state of mind. If they are in a state of panic be very cautious and try to calm them, because they are liable to cause you to upset, in which case you will be in the water with them.

Photo 27 - Flat water canoe recovery. The person in the water can help by swimming forward, pushing the canoe ahead. This recovery is easy to do in calm water, but in the wind and waves is another thing.

You will need assistance of only one person in the water, and can do without that if necessary. If there are two people in the water, have one of them go to the stern of your canoe and hold on to both gunwales to help stabilize it. If the capsized canoe is right side up, have the other person turn it over and then swim to the far end and push down which will lift the other end (the end nearest you) and break the suction. Then pull the upside down canoe over your canoe until it is completely out of the water resting on your canoe's gunwales. The swimmer can assist with this, although it is not a difficult to do it by yourself. Once the canoe is clear of the water, turn it right side up and slide it back into the water.

With the canoe alongside yours, hang on firmly to the gunwales of both canoes and have the people in the water get into their canoe. Continue to hang on to the canoe until they have their paddles and can handle the canoe by themselves. If necessary, assist in recovering gear that may still be floating.

Seldom is a flat water rescue as serious as one in whitewater, but the wind and waves can greatly add to the difficulty. If it is early or late season then hypothermia of the victims is a real concern and then the speed of the recovery becomes critical. Never underestimate the seriousness of any upset. Better to be overcautious than to make a critical mistake.

Using a Motor: With a simple, but rugged, side mount a

moderate or large canoe can be turned into a handy and versatile motorboat. A 20 foot canoe will easily handle a six horsepower outboard and will push the canoe in excess of 10 miles per hour with a moderate load. I have clocked my own twenty foot canoe at 10 miles per hour (with a GPS) using only a four horsepower engine.

Many people think of a square stern canoe when they are considering using power, but that is not necessary. The side mount has few disadvantages and offers the advantage of allowing you to quickly convert back to a sleek hand powered craft. Of course the side-mounted motor will cause an empty canoe to list seriously when floating and you must take that into consideration. However, this is easily overcome by loading the canoe properly. Even an empty canoe with one or two occupants is easily balanced by simply shifting the people's weight to one side.

A motor can be an emergency item on a paddling trip. It will allow the leader to move quickly for help in an emergency, either with or against the current. Many folks will appreciate the security of having a motor along even if it gets a free ride the entire trip. It may be that your guests look forward to paddling a river portion of a trip, but dislike the lake paddling. You can take them in tow and cross the lakes at leisure.

When towing it is important that you get the weight in the towed canoes further back than would be normal for paddling. The towed canoes should ride with the bows high. If this is not done the canoes will switch back and forth and could capsize if allowed to go too far and too fast.

A canoe motor is not for everyone, but it does make the worlds most versatile boat even more versatile.

Just as the early Europeans quickly recognized the value of the canoe, so do knowledgeable outdoor people. Today the canoe is considered a pleasure craft by most people, but it is still a valuable tool for people who spend a lot of time in the outdoors. Trappers, hunters, explorers, photographers, writers - name an outdoor activity and most likely you will find a canoe being used by the people involved in it.

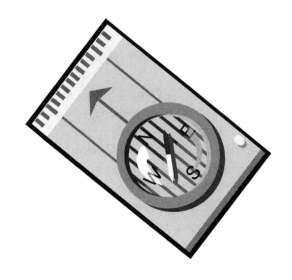

Land Navigation

This is not intended to be a course in map and compass. There are some good books available that cover the subject much more thoroughly than I possible could in one chapter in this book. What I do wish to get across are some of the shortcomings I have noted in observing people use maps, compasses, and GPS receivers. I have served for several years on the Board for the Licensing of Guides in Maine. Part of the guide testing process is oral testing in the use of map and compass. What I plan to cover here are the most common mistakes I have observed in my capacity as an examiner and also as a guide using map and compass in the field. Hopefully this will give you, the outdoor leader, a heads-up on subjects that are important to master as you study, and put into practice, map and compass skills.

I first learned about reading topographic (topo) maps in the military. As a cavalry officer, sometimes moving my unit long distances over unfamiliar terrain, map reading skills were mandatory. That training served me well later on when I became a professional guide. Many things are the same as what I learned back then, but there have been some important changes in the years since then that have made land navigation easier and more accurate.

The two most important advances, since those days so long ago, are the base plate compass and the Global Positioning System receivers. The base plate compass is actually two tools in one. The most obvious is that it is a magnetic compass, but the other is that it can function as a protractor. The Global Positioning Receiver, or GPS as it is commonly known, has revolutionized land, water and air navigation. While it is not mandatory knowledge for the outdoor leader, as is map and compass, it is becoming an important tool and the serious outdoor leader should become proficient in its use.

There are a number of books that cover the subject of land navigation. Three that I have used are listed below. They are all available from amazon.com and most book stores can order them for you if they do not stock them.

Be Expert With Map and Compass, *The Complete Orienteering Handbook* by Bjorn Hjellstrom seems to be the standard text for those involved in the sport of orienteering, and it is a valuable text for the modern day land navigator as well. It has good explanations of the language of maps as well as clear lessons in the use of the base plate compass.

GPS Made Easy, *Using Global Positioning Systems in the Outdoors* by Lawrence Letham is excellent for anyone wishing to learn about using GPS. My first trial with GPS was a disaster, in fact I ended up returning it for a refund in disgust, because I could see no advantage of it over my compass. At that time the only written instruction I had was the manufacturer's booklet that came with the instrument - very inadequate. A year or so later I learned our game wardens were being equipped with GPS receivers. If the wardens were using them, I decided, there must be something I had missed with the first try and so I bought another one and the above book. I have been an enthusiastic GPS user ever since.

One of the most important features of this book is the clear explanation of the various grid systems used on topographic maps. The most important of these, for the land navigator, are Latitude/ Longitude and the Universal Transverse Mercator (UTM) grid.

Wilderness Navigation, *Finding Your Way Using Map, Compass, Altimeter & GPS* by Bob Burns and Mike Burns. As the title implies, this book gives a more broad brush treatment to the subject of land navigation and seems to presume the reader has some basic knowledge of topo maps. It is written more for the hiker than for a general outdoor audience.

Bearing and Azimuth: The words "bearing" and "azimuth" are commonly used interchangeably. I found this to be true even in the books on map and compass. There is a difference in the two, however, and you should know about it whichever term you use. Correctly used, azimuth is expressed as 0 to 360 degrees whereas bearing is measured from the cardinal directions of north or south and would be expressed as, for example: S45°W which would be an azimuth of 225°. We have found that certain professions, such as foresters, are trained in the use of bearings, probably for their survey work. To avoid possible confusion I have used the correct word, azimuth, exclusively. However you will find the word "bearing" used in other texts with the same meaning as I described above for azimuth.

The Language of Maps: In order to use and understand topo maps it is necessary to first learn their language. You could say that three languages are used, English (the written word), colors and symbols. Since you are reading this you already are familiar with one of the languages. Colors are easy to remember because they are common sense - blue for water, green for vegetation, etc. The most common symbols are common sense too - a little house for a building, put a cross on it and you have a church, etc. But there are some that are a little more obscure and are not seen on every map sheet you may look at.

The outdoor leader should especially pay attention to those symbols that represent natural features, since he or she will not be operating where there are a lot of man-made objects. Contour lines (brown) are an important feature to understand. They tell you the elevation above sea level, the shape of the terrain around you and also can tell you which way a stream is flowing.

Declination: This important part of land navigation confuses more people than any other aspect. Both Burns' and Hjellstrom's books explain with diagrams what and why we have declination as well as how to apply it to map reading.

Since magnetic north can be 18 or 20 degrees, or more, different from true or grid north in the United States, it is vital that the outdoor leader be aware of it and allow for it whenever using map and compass. You should know why there *is* declination and why, for example, there is zero declination somewhere in Wisconsin and some other states in the middle of the country.

The problem most people have is knowing whether to add or subtract the declination to arrive at the north they are seeking. You will have to devise your own system for remembering, but I'll tell you mine. I just remember that the word "magnetic" is larger than the word "true". Therefore the magnetic azimuth will be larger than the true azimuth. Of course this only applies in the eastern part of the country where I live. Westerners could apply the opposite logic or come up with another system. Another thing to remember is that there are 360 degrees in a circle. So if the declination is west 10 degrees, and the true azimuth is 355 degrees, then adding 10 degrees to get the magnetic azimuth, results in an azimuth of 5 degrees, not the impossible azimuth of 365 degrees.

There is also another declination that will appear on topo maps. That is the UTM grid declination. Grid north can vary slightly from true north, but usually it is a variance of less than one degree and can be disregarded in practical land navigation.

Some of the base plate compasses are constructed so that declination can be applied automatically. I personally find this to be more confusing than adding or subtracting it, but for someone else it may be just the thing.

Map Grids: I never fully understood the UTM grid system until I read Letham's GPS book. He also covers the Latitude/Longitude grid which most everyone is familiar with since it is used world-wide. There are other grids in use, but these two are the most common and are most used by land navigators.

This is a very simplified explanation, but the basic difference in the two grids is as follows: The latitude/longitude grid is based on the fact that the earth is a sphere, and the measurements are in degrees, minutes and seconds. Latitude lines are parallel to the equator and are designated North (N) or South (S) with the equator being zero. Longitude lines run from pole to pole with Greenwich, England being the prime meridian with a designation of zero. The other meridians are designated West (W) or East (E) of the prime meridian. A lat/long coordinate is usually written hemisphere latitude, hemisphere longitude like this; N 47° 19.56', E 102° 42.84'. This is called a geographic coordinate because it is based on a sphere.

The UTM grid is arrived at by artificially flattening the world and dividing it up into 60 zones which are 6° wide. Each zone has a meridian in the center and metric measurements are taken from it. These are called eastings. The easting can increase (East) from the central meridian or decrease (West). Northings in the UTM grid are measured in meters North and South of the equator.

Once mastered the UTM grid is easy to use in the field. Eastings and northings can be read directly from the map without the aid of a ruler, and accurately to within a few meters. Even more accurate if you use a ruler. I have plotted known points on the map, like crossroads, then entered the coordinates into my GPS. I was almost right on when I arrived. Try it, it will make a believer of you.

Common Sense: A frequent mistake by people plotting an azimuth on a map is to be 180 degrees off. What they do is place their base plate compass on the map with the direction arrow pointing the opposite direction from that which they wish to travel. The common sense factor is not used and they fail the test or, even worse if in real life, they end up going straight away from where they want to go.

The first thing to do after laying out a course on a map is to imagine the four cardinal directions to see what ballpark your

100   *The Outdoor Leader's Handbook*

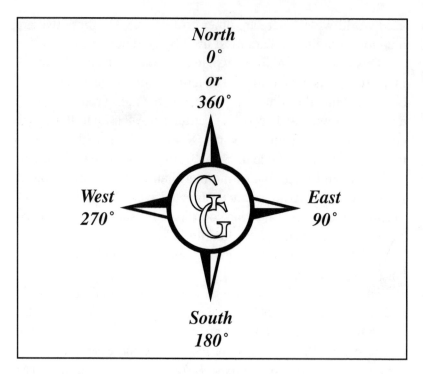

Figure 7 - **The compass rose. Imagine this in your mind as you lay out a course. You will always know if you are in the ballpark.**

azimuth will be. The cardinal directions are shown in Figure 7. Now just look at the direction you have to travel and, keeping the compass rose in mind, judge which cardinal direction it is closest to. If the course of travel is generally east then the azimuth you come up with should be somewhere in the vicinity of 90 degrees. If your direction is somewhere south of due east then the azimuth will be more than 90, but less than 180. But if you come up with something closer to 270 than to 90, then something is wrong and you better re-think the thing.

By using common sense and doing a quick estimate of your azimuth before putting the compass or protractor on the map you will always be able to check your own work.

Orienting a Map: It is possible to plot a route from one place to another on a map and read the compass direction you will have to travel to get there. One way is to line up the compass on the

Photo 28 - **Maine Game Warden Micah Thurston using his base plate compass as a protractor on the hood of his truck.**

map and rotate the map and compass until the compass needle points north; then the map is oriented to north. At this point the azimuth can be read from the compass.

The problem with orienting the map magnetically is that there can always be compass variations that will thrown you off a few degrees one way or another. Another thing is that it is not always easy to find a flat surface, away from anything that might effect the compass, to do the magnetic orientation.

A big advantage to the base plate compass is that it can be used as a protractor. Both of the map and compass books I mentioned show how to do this. With this method there is no need to orient the map to get an accurate reading and it can be done on the hood of a truck or any other convenient surface. Once the azimuth to the destination is determined all that is left is to convert the reading to magnetic so you can follow a magnetic compass course, and you are ready to go. You do this, of course, by adding (East) or subtracting (West) the declination.

As mentioned before, a common mistake is to read the wrong end of the magnetic needle. Usually the north pointing end is red. Be sure you are reading the correct end or you will be 180° off. This would make it a loooong trip.

Back Azimuth: My friend, Dick, and also one of the Guide Board examiners, told me this story about one of the candidates he tested. The person wasn't doing very well, and the score was marginal - maybe pass, maybe not. Dick noticed that the candidate seemed to be a name and phrase dropper using some of them several times as the oral exam proceeded.

One of the candidate's favorite phrases to drop was "back azimuth" it came up so many times that Dick became suspicious. He asked the candidate to explain what "back azimuth" meant. It turned out the candidate didn't have a clue, but apparently thought it was important and would impress somebody if used often enough. The candidate failed.

Back azimuth is simple. It is 180° from the original azimuth. If the original azimuth is less than 180° then add 180°. If the original course was more than 180°, then subtract 180°.

There is a lot of satisfaction in being able to navigate with map, compass, and now, GPS. I remember near the end of our map and compass training when I was in the army. After weeks of classroom work, we were given a map and compass along with a list of coordinates. We plotted the coordinates on our maps, determined the magnetic azimuth to follow and set off through the woods to find each plotted points. Each coordinate was a check point which we had to check into before proceeding to the next one. When I successfully completed the course I remember thinking to myself, *I'll be damned, it really works.*

Dealing *with* *Weather*

When most people imagine an outdoor adventure their mind's eye sees warm, sunny and calm days. This seldom happens unless the person is very lucky or is only out for a day or two. This Pollyanna attitude sometimes causes them to leave home without the proper clothing and equipment for adverse weather. As the outdoor leader it is up to you to be sure to stress the importance of them having the clothing and equipment that you have specified.

I have had people show up for a week long canoe trip with a rain suit that cost less than $5.00. Those plastic suits are a waste of money and at best they will protect someone for a one time wearing, and then only if they are careful and don't wear it too long. If a prolonged period of wet weather comes along they are without protection. If there is the possibility of cold weather where you will be operating it is equally important to ensure your guests have warm clothing and doubly important they have proper rain gear. I had a situation that could have been a real problem on one late season trip.

It was late September and the canoe trip was in northern Maine. Weather at this time of year can range from summer-like to very winter-like. The day we started our trip the temperature was in the eighties and we worked at loading our canoes in our tee shirts. We were ready to shove off, and as I headed for my canoe with one of the young people in my party he casually remarked he was leaving his coat in the truck, implying there was no need for it given the weather at hand. I immediately made him go get it and proceeded to check that the others had theirs. That trip proved to be one of the coldest I had ever experienced with everything from freezing temperatures to heavy, wet snow that threatened to collapse our tents. That youngster was very thankful that he had mentioned leaving his coat behind and that I had insisted he go back for it.

Every season and activity has its own weather dangers and the outdoor leader must know what the worst can be, and prepare for it. This means to prepare yourself as well as to ensure your guests are prepared. If you decide to stay put because of weather conditions then do it; even if it means spending extra days afield beyond what was planned. It is better for one of your guests to miss a day of work than to be part of a disaster. Always pack extra supplies for just such an emergency. Explain the situation to the guests, and do not let their uninformed judgement sway you into doing something against *your* better judgement.

Predicting the weather is something that my guests always thought I, as a Master Maine Guide, should be good at. I never thought I was, but I learned that I was better than most of them. That meant I was the best they had around. I could recognize many of the signs of approaching weather, but I had a trick I used too. I would pay close attention to the long range forecast just before the trip. The weather service posts them nearly a week ahead, and they are fairly reliable, at least for the first three or four days out. When asked, I could give what I remembered and look pretty good in their eyes. It is kind of like the old Indian guide who forecasted the next days weather and got it exactly right every time. His people were really impressed with the old mans native ability to read weather signs. Then one day he didn't have a forecast for them. Nothing! When asked why he replied, "My radio broke".

The old-timers used rhymes to help them remember, and pass on, weather signs. In fact, old time outdoorsmen and farmers were quite good at short-range weather forcasting. Every one of the rhymes has an element of truth about weather that is to come. One many folks have heard of is:

> Red sky at night, sailor's delight;
> Red sky at morning, sailors take warning.

Another version of this one is:

> Evening red and morning gray,
> Help the traveler on his way;
> Evening gray and morning red,
> Bring down rain upon his head.

The dew on the grass, or lack of it, is a pretty good indication of the weather to come. For rain:

> When grass is dry at morning light,
> Look for rain before the night;
> When the grass is dry at night,
> Look for rain before the light.

For fair weather:

> When the dew is on the grass,
> Rain will never come to pass.

There's a rhyme for fog too:

> Evening fog will not burn soon,
> Morning fog will burn 'fore noon.

The wind is one of the best forecasting tools for the outdoorsman:

> When the wind is in the south,
> The rain is in its mouth.

We know our weather travels west to east, and low pressure systems rotate counter-clockwise, highs clockwise, so:

> When the wind is in the east,
> 'Tis fit for neither man nor beast!

And:

> When the wind is in the west,
> There it is the very best.

This rhyme uses clouds as a predictor of winds to come:

> Mackerel scales and mares' tails
> Make lofty ships carry low sails.

I wouldn't want to bet the farm on any of these rhymes being 100% accurate, but they are a good indicator and make us aware of things that do precede changes in the weather. There *is* some scientific foundation for each of them. Changes in weather are changes in the atmosphere. These rhymes simply point out those changes and what they mean. The outdoor leader should watch and learn what the various signs bring on in her/his area. Sometimes what is coming for weather in a day or two can have a significant effect on plans for that period of time.

Rain: This is the most common adverse weather that the outdoor leader has to deal with. If she/he is properly prepared, and has properly prepared the guests, it should be no serious problem in any kind of outing. In the Camping chapter I talked about shelters and it is important that they be used whenever there is rain or threat of it. A guest who gets his clothing and gear totally soaked is a real problem, especially if the weather is cool. Hypothermia is possible even during the warm summer months. If it happens it is up to the leader to somehow get the person dry and keep him/her warm. However, prevention is much better then the cure. Keep 'em dry!

If the rain is heavy you may want to alter plans accordingly or go into an alternate plan for whatever your activity may be. There are few things that we do in the out-of-doors that cannot be done in the rain. Whether or not people will be enthusiastic about doing them is another matter. Postponing some activities is just common sense.

We were ready to run the hardest rapids of our trip. Rain came in heavy overnight and showed no signs of let-up in the morning. I decided to wait a day to continue our trip and the white-water run. The reason for my decision was that if anyone upset in the rapids and got wet, it would be very difficult to get them dry and warm in the pouring rain. Better to put it off a day and make the lost time up later.

People who are prepared will have a good time regardless of the weather. I remember two twin boys, about 5 years old, on a canoe trip with their parents. We were getting heavy rain, and since we had time to spare, we decided to lay over a day and wait it out. The boys were well equipped with quality rain gear and all day long they played in the rain. The sound of them, squealing and laughing, having such a good time was cheering to all of us. One of the things they thought was great fun was standing under the stream of water coming off the tarp that was covering our dining area.

Heavy rains can cause wash-outs and create high water in streams and rivers that can cause a real problem to people traveling in wild areas. This type of problem most frequently happens in the spring time, but can occur in any season. When this happens the outdoor leader has to use judgement and common sense in dealing with the problem. His or her first consideration has to always be the safety and well being of his guests. Every other consideration is secondary.

Wind: The dangers from wind will depend on the level it is blowing. For many activities it has little effect, at least when it is blowing at a reasonable rate. However, if you are doing anything on the water pay close attention to the wind. Know how to judge its danger and be prepared to deal with it.

I was camped on a lee shore of a large lake and our route of travel for the day would take us across the lake. I awoke in the morning to the sound of wind blowing through the trees and I knew then we might be forced to stay put for the day, or until the wind died down. The lake in front of our camp was deceptively calm, but I could look out at a distance and see white caps rolling down the lake. Some of my guests could not understand why I insisted we remain where we were. All they could see was the nice calm water in front of our camp. Some were a little put-out that we could not get under way, but I had to insist we remain where we were. Decisions like those are hard, but they are part of taking care of people in a wilderness situation.

Take care if anyone gets wet on a windy day. The wind chill increases the chance of hypothermia even though it feels quite warm when you are dry. Insist they get into dry clothing as soon as possible. The symptoms of hypothermia begin on Page 114.

Thunderstorms: Both wind and rain along with lightening and sometimes hail can be expected with these dangerous storms. No matter what your outdoor activity may be it is important you show thunderstorms a lot of respect. Preparation for a thunderstorm demands that you recognize that one is on the way.

Electrical storms, like other weather systems, travel from west to east. So, if you use your compass and draw and imaginary east-west line through your position you can determine if a storm on the horizon will travel over your position. If your line goes through the approaching storm, or a little south of it, you should prepare for it to pass over your position. If you hear or see storms to your south or far north they will probably not effect you directly. Also, storms heard to the east of your position have already gone by. They do not turn around and come back. When this seems to be the case it is a second storm, rather than the first

Photo 29 - **The classic anvil-shaped cloud. A warning of approaching danger that the outdoor leader should take seriously.**

one returning. Even if the storms you can see or hear are no threat to your position it pays to be prepared. Whenever storms are in the area, there can still be one out there with your position in its sights. Sound travels about a mile in five seconds. If you see lightening and count off five seconds before you hear thunder, the storm is one mile away.

Learn to recognize approaching storms as well as the type of weather that breeds them. When you see cumulus clouds piling up to great heights in the western sky you should expect to have storms around in the next few hours. Those thunder heads are sometimes described as anvil-shaped, being wider at the top than the rest of the formation. They do not always take that shape, however.

If you are on the water when a storm is approaching get off as soon as possible. Head for an area that will offer protection from the wind and get your boats or canoes high and dry to protect them from pounding waves. Wherever you are with a storm approaching, get the people inland and avoid trees or other objects that are taller than the surrounding vegetation. If even-size evergreens are close by they will afford protection from heavy rain and hail as well as shelter from the wind. Be sure there are no widow-makers (trees or branches that could come down) in the vicinity. High winds make them doubly dangerous. If possible put up a tarp for people to get under. I usually do not allow people to sit on their personal floatation devices (PFD's), but in an electrical storm sitting or kneeling on them will give some degree of protection from lightening. It also gets people down low which is the safest place to be. A good rule of thumb for lightening protection is to avoid being the tallest thing in your surroundings.

This little story illustrates how the outdoor leader has to cope with conditions in a manner a little different from what is considered conventional wisdom. We have all heard the TV weatherman warn us to seek cover indoors when thunderstorms threaten. But, this is not an easy task when the nearest thing to indoors is the nylon walls of a tent or the cover of a tarp.

We were on a seven day trip on the Allagash Wilderness Waterway. The trip started with hot, humid weather punctuated with occasional thunderstorms. By midway through the trip the thunderstorms had increased to a regular progression of them. In over thirty years of canoe trips I had never seen so many in a short period of time. Still, we managed to cope and most of the time were able to travel between the storms and to have our camp set up before the next batch bore down upon us.

When we finished the trip and returned home we learned that the folks back home had heard about our storms. They told us the TV weatherman had warned Allagash travelers to find shelter in a cabin because of the severe storms. I had to laugh at the ignorance of those weathermen about the conditions of wilderness travel. First off, we could never have heard their warnings because there was no television. Secondly, there are no cabins located along the route just for the care and comfort of wilderness travelers. We dealt with the storms with common sense along with a knowledge of what to do to minimize the dangers. Just part of the job for the outdoor leader.

Hot Weather: Operating outdoors during hot weather can be dangerous for people who are not used to dealing with those conditions. You should watch your guests closely for signs of sunburn, heat exhaustion and sunstroke. Encourage them to use sunscreen on all exposed skin, and if you see evidence of sunburn, have them cover up with clothing immediately. You should also learn to recognize heat exhaustion and sunstroke.

The symptoms of heat exhaustion are profuse sweating, pale skin - clammy to the touch, and the person will seem disoriented, weak and rather anxious. If you observe these symptoms have the person lie down in a cool place with his head slightly lower than the rest of the body. Apply ice or cold packs to the face, neck, arms and shoulders. Give cool water to drink and monitor the situation until the symptoms disappear.

If you observe someone with the face and body flushed and the skin is hot and dry, you have a case of sunstroke. The pupils will be enlarged and the person will be behaving strangely. Sunstroke can be very serious and you should make plans to evacuate the victim as soon as possible. In the meantime, get him or her into a cool area, apply ice or cold water packs to the face, neck, arms and shoulders. If the victim remains conscious give cool drink in small quantities. Give no stimulants! You, or someone, should monitor the victim constantly until relieved by medical professionals.

Cold Weather - Winter Conditions: In the past, for many people, winter was the forgotten season for outdoor activities. That has changed in the past 30 or 40 years, and now there is a lot of interest in seeing the wilderness under its cloak of snow and ice. Unfortunately many of those people venturing into the wilds are ill informed and ill equipped to be there. It is a season of sudden weather changes and one that can be unforgiving of mistakes. Not only unforgiving of mistakes, but swift to punish anyone who makes one.

It is the outdoor leader's job to ensure the people he takes out on any cold-weather activity are well prepared for it. This means adequate clothing, layered and of the right type for the activity. The leader must also have knowledge of the area so no one blunders into something serious.

During the spring and fall, the seasons of change, it is often hard to convince people that winter can, and often does, intrude

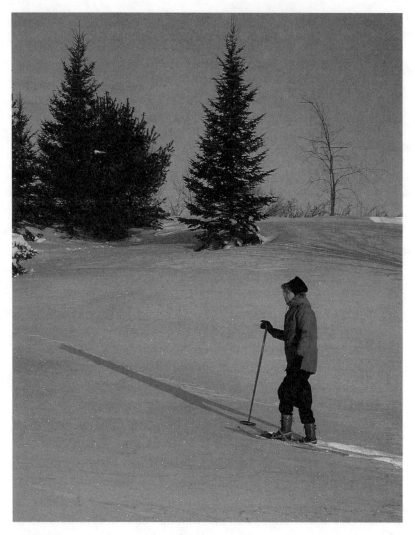

Photo 30 - **Winter is a great time to be outdoors - as long as you are prepared for it.**

into these seasons. When it does it can be even more dangerous than it is in its own season unless you are prepared for it. The youngster who was leaving his coat behind is a good example.

If a person falls through the ice when the temperature is zero or below, you have only minutes to take action. The first thing is to get the person out of the water, of course. Next, a decision has to be made. How far from home or camp? Is the victim physically able to get there quickly. Should you build a fire right there, strip the wet clothing off the victim and try to warm him on the spot? Every situation will be different, but there isn't a lot of time to decide, so it is best to think about it ahead of time.

If you take people out on a multiple day trip with winter camping overnight it is important to be aware of the weather and what can happen. Heavy, unexpected snowstorms can come along and alter your plans. A whiteout can make navigation difficult or impossible. Tents and other gear that are perfectly adequate for summer camping my not stand up to the hardships of cold weather. People must be observed closely for frostbite, hypothermia and exhaustion, all problems that can be brought on by extremely cold weather.

Frostbite: The guests must be watched closely for signs of frostbite. It can happen is a short period of time and can be painful. It will certainly ruin their day. Frostbite is the freezing of body tissue. It effects the exposed skin like the nose, cheeks, ears and the hands and feet in extreme cold conditions. The victim often experiences a tingling feeling and the frostbitten part will feel hard to the touch. The skin will be gray or white.

As long as the frostbite is not too deep, that is, superficial, it can be warmed by covering the part with warm hands, or if it is the hands, by placing then in the armpits. Do not try to re-warm frostbitten parts with water, or anything else, above 98.6° Fahrenheit. Take care of frostbite as soon as it is discovered to prevent a more serious problem.

Severe frostbite is a very serious problem that the outdoor leader should be on guard against. It is when there is solid freezing of tissues. Just how serious the problem, is for medical people to determine, but treatment is almost always beyond the ability of persons in the field. In fact more damage can be done. The best thing the outdoor leader can do in this situation is to prevent further freezing and do everything possible to evacuate the victim for medical treatment.

Like any other problem in the outdoors, prevention is the best medicine. The careful, vigilant leader will seldom have people with frostbite because he or she is takes steps to ensure it doesn't happen.

Hypothermia: It used to be called simply "exposure". It is a lowered body temperature, and that can mean trouble when there is no warm, centrally heated house to retreat into at the first sign of a shiver or chill.

Out internal organs are designed to function at 98.6° Fahrenheit. Any variation in this temperature can cause trouble. A difference of as little as 1/2 degree can cause illness - fever or chills. A difference of five degrees is a threat to life itself. The good news for the cold weather adventurer is that the body is more tolerant of lower temperatures than higher ones.

Hypothermia can occur at *any* time of the year if conditions are right. It is brought on by exhaustion and overexposure to cold and wet. When this happens the body's heat is lost faster than it is produced. The body responds by making involuntary adjustments to preserve the normal temperature of internal organs. This results in reduced blood flow to the extremities, and exercise is needed for the person to stay warm. Of course, the exhausted person is not anxious to start exercising. In these circumstances the person often loses clarity of judgment, which just makes matters worse as they may resist treatment.

The leader should learn to spot hypothermia in its early stages so that immediate steps can be taken. The following symptoms should not be ignored:
- Uncontrollable shivering
- Slurred speech, slow speech, vagueness
- Lapse in memory
- Immobility , fumbling
- Stumbling and lurching
- Drowsiness
- Exhaustion

The condition of the hypothermia victim as listed here according to body temperature will give some idea of just how serious this thing can be:

98.6 - 91 degrees: Shivering becomes intense, difficult tasks are hard to perform.

91 - 86 degrees: Shivering decreases, muscle rigidity sets in. Poor muscle coordination and total amnesia may be present.

86 - 81 degrees: The victim becomes irrational and drifts into a stupor.

81 - 78 degrees: Heart becomes erratic. Most reflexes cease to function. The victim becomes unconscious.

Below 78 degrees: Cardiac and respiratory arrest occur, causing death.

Like other problems in the outdoors, prevention is the best cure. Ensure that people stay warm and dry and are not at or close to exhaustion. The leader always has to be aware that guests frequently do not have the stamina that he or she may possess. Stress the need for warm clothing and the importance of staying dry. Clothing for cold or cool weather should be wool or fleece that will provide insulation even when wet.

Keep a supply of high energy snacks available for cold weather - candy, nuts, raisins, etc. can be just the fuel that the body's furnace needs to keep producing life-giving heat. Make up a large batch of hot chocolate for folks to sip. It supplies heat and energy at the same time.

If it becomes necessary to treat someone for hypothermia, start by getting them out of wet clothing and into dry ones. Give the person warm, sweet liquids to drink and supply an external heat source. This source could be a warm fire, warm rocks placed around the sleeping bag, or another person, a heat donor, inside the bag with the victim. Both naked is best.

If you suspect advanced hypothermia, do everything listed above, and then start determining how to evacuate the victim to a doctor or medical facility.

Finally, don't ignore yourself in your concern for your guests! One of the symptoms of hypothermia is *impaired judgement*! You must be able to think clearly to do your job. So, it is as important for your guest's welfare that you take care of yourself as it is for you to care for them

It is impossible to list all of the challenges that may be brought on by the weather, but the outdoor leader can be prepared mentally, and have proper equipment, to deal with whatever may come along. It is always best to err on the side of safety! It will not always please your guests, but at least they'll be alive and well to complain about it.

You have a
Lost Person!

If you find yourself in the position of being responsible for the welfare of others in an outdoor situation you should be realize how awesome this responsibility can be. It doesn't matter if you are a parent on a family outing, a camp councilor on a canoe trip, an adult scout leader on a 50 mile hike or a paid licensed guide on a hunting trip. You are responsible to see that everyone gets home safe and sound.

This chapter will give the general guidelines to use in, at first preventing anyone from getting lost, and then, if lost, how to find them. There are no hard and fast rules here because every situation will be different. What the following will do is give you some things to consider and to apply to each situation as it might occur. Differences in people, terrain, activity, weather, and other factors will have an effect on the leaders reaction to situations that arise.

Pre-briefing: The best way to handle the possibility that someone in your care may become lost is to ensure it will not happen. This is best done by planning ahead, way ahead. This prior planning begins as soon as the trip is initiated. Find out all you can about the people in your party. If they have health problems, special food needs or other special considerations, you need to know about them. This is important even outside the possibility they may become lost. It is also helpful to know the approximate age of everyone. This is sometimes a touchy subject to bring up as it might imply age discrimination to some people. Nevertheless it can be handled diplomatically. Perhaps by having them indicate an age group they fall into such as: 30 - 40, 40 - 50, etc. I have found that most people of advanced age or with a serious disability were anxious for me to know it up front. Of course if the people in your party are family or friends then you will probably have all the information you need without digging for it.

Prior to departing your home base for the activity you have planned it is a good idea to sit down with everyone concerned and go over the area you will be operating in. Use a map and indicate the boundaries that might be easily remembered and recognized. Even if the people are not familiar with topographic maps, they can recognize the features if you point them out. Be sure to emphasize how large the area might be regardless of how small it appears on the map. Do this by estimating and telling them how long it would take to walk from one side to the other, or by comparing it to something the guest can relate to, such as city blocks. This briefing will also give you a chance to evaluate your guests knowledge of maps and the use of a compass. Use this information to decide whether they should be carrying them.

As elemental as it may seem, it is important to impress upon everyone how to know if they are lost. Tell them in no uncertain terms that if they do not know how to get back to the camp, truck, or wherever they started from, then they are lost and should accept that fact. At that realization they should stay put and wait for you to find them. To do otherwise will only result in complications which will translate to them remaining in the woods alone for a lot longer than would otherwise be the case. A good analogy to use is that in the first hour or so the search area can be represented by the size of a common business card. A few hours later it is the size of an open newspaper.

Tell them that a lost person can get busy while they are remaining in place. First, instruct them to look for the most open area in their immediate vicinity. This will allow an aircraft to spot them if the search has to reach that stage. If they have something bright like blaze orange, be sure it is visible from the air. Anything, including their face, that will contrast with the surroundings will make them easier to spot. Next they should gather wood for a fire. The fire will do wonders for their state of mind and, of course, it will act as a signal for searchers. Tell them to gather enough wood to last all night. When they think they have enough they should gather that much more. Point out that green evergreen boughs added to the fire from time to time will produce a very good signal smoke. Also name some good fire starters such as birch bark, dry punk, small dead branches, etc. Demonstrate using these as you build your fires when the trip gets under way.

A good friend of mine found it necessary to spend the night in the woods. He had been given the wrong compass direction to return to camp and made the mistake of not checking it out for himself. By the time he realized something was wrong it was too late to get out before dark. He built a fire and spent the night in relative comfort. When morning came he built the fire up and sat back and waited to be found. He was near a lake, and a Warden plane soon landed to take him out. The pilot told him that he saw the smoke from the fire as soon as he was airborne.

Once the fire is going the lost person should be told to make himself as visible as possible and to listen for the rescuer. He/she should be listening for a pre-arranged signal. If it is a hunting trip the signal can be shots fired. Perhaps three evenly spaced shots by the lost person with two as an answer by the rescuer. If no firearms are in use then whistles should be used, again with a pre-arranged number. Impress on the people that if darkness overtakes them that it will not stop your search. In fact, darkness simplifies the search because signals are easier to hear, especially signal shots, which at night are not likely to be confused with shots fired at game.

During this pre-trip briefing it is important to impress on everyone what they can do to prevent being lost in the first place. The situations that might cause one to become lost will vary with the activity and the area you are dealing with. Canoe trips on most of the waterways in Maine are actually through working commercial forests. I always warned people to avoid getting on wood hauling roads that came close to where we camped. Roads, to people not woods-wise, are associated with civilization. Not so in the working forest. They may lead to nowhere and finally peter out leaving one with nowhere to go. Finally impress on everyone that if they do get lost the most important thing they can do to ensure their own safety is to follow the rules covered above and **not to panic**. Panic has killed More lost people in the woods than any other cause. Make them believe that you have the ability and the determination to find them if it becomes necessary.

Your pre-briefing should also include making sure your guests have the clothing and equipment needed for the area and season you are dealing with. In addition, insist that at a minimum they carry the following items with them at all times:

Waterproof matches and/or a disposable lighter
Spare ammunition (hunting trip) and a whistle for signaling
Map (Depending on qualifications)
Compass (Depending on qualifications)
Personal medicine and glasses
Emergency food
A knife
Water and/or water purification tablets

You can either require people to bring these items with them or you may want to furnish them. You can also add to this list depending on the situation. Clothing your guests wear and take along should be adequate for the worst weather possible for the season. This is something that should not be taken lightly by you because your guests may have no experience to draw upon regarding the climate in your area. Talk to them about it, and as diplomatically as possible, get them to describe what they have with them. If you are dealing with young people it is a good idea to have a look at the items.

If your guests are going to be carrying a map and compass be sure that they have sufficient knowledge to use them. At a minimum be sure they understand how to reverse course to return to a road, or whatever, that they started out from. Make them aware of the direction any flowing water in the area will be running as well as any recognizable landmarks. This will allow for a quick orientation if one should become confused. Point out anything that could cause confusion or lead to more trouble. Point out the dangers of following a woods road which may not lead to where they want to go even though it initially appears to do so.

On a river canoe trip in northern Maine a young lady in my party became lost. She, along with everyone else, had been briefed on the woods roads, stream direction and all the rest. As it turned out she got lost because she ignored my warning about the woods roads, but found her way out by remembering what I said about the stream flow direction. She kept her head and figured out that the stream she came across would lead her to the river. She finally came to the river's edge about a mile from our campsite and was spotted making her way toward our camp. It is hard to say who was happier, her to be back or me to have her back safe and well.

It is important to equip yourself for the possibility of a search for a lost person. Put together a kit to include, at a minimum, the following items: I assume an outdoor leader would always have a knife and matches or lighter on his/her person. If that is not the case for you then add them to the following list. (And, get in the habit of carrying them all the time.)

Flashlight with extra bulb and batteries,
Rescue blanket,
Basic first aid kit
Plastic marking tape
A topographic map of the area

A compass

A global positioning system receiver - (GPS)

A whistle

Extra ammunition (if a hunting trip)

A pencil and notebook

Emergency food

Water and/or water purification tablets

Have these items in a pack that you can quickly pick up and commence your search, should it become necessary. It is a good idea to have the phone numbers of people and agencies that you may have to call in an emergency.

An often heard phrase these days is, "knowledge is power". Keep it in mind as you brief your guests, because the more they know the less likely they will become lost. And, if they do get lost, will be better able to care for themselves until help arrives. This in turn will make your life a lot simpler and more enjoyable.

The Search: There is a good reason why professionals, like fire fighters, policemen, wardens, emergency medical technicians (EMT's) and others involved in the business of rescuing people spend so much time training. It is so they know exactly what to do without thinking about it in times of extreme stress. For the outdoor leader there is nothing more stressful than finding out one of his/her charges is lost. From my own experience I can tell you that it felt like someone kicked me in the stomach. and then this was followed by a panicked feeling of wanting to race into the woods to find the individual right then and there. This is the point where training and discipline take over and allow you to do the right thing.

It isn't necessary to lose someone in the woods to train yourself. It *is* a good idea, working with other outdoor leaders if possible, to do some training and go through the steps that need to be taken. At the very least the outdoor leader should have thought through the things he/she will do in the event of a lost person in their party. Having a sequence of events thought out ahead of time will prevent panic and allow you to do the right thing.

Once it is determined that someone is lost you should first

think about the rest of your party. Every situation will be different, but your first consideration has to be making sure no one else becomes lost. Do this by insisting they stay in camp, or wherever, and remain there no matter what. Give them something to do like keeping a fire going, listening for the pre-arranged signals, and preparing their own meals while you are searching. Anything that will keep them safely occupied will calm them down and this will help alleviate some of your worries.

It will often happen that a close friend or relative of the lost person is a part of your party. That person will be emotionally involved and probably want to help with the search. In nearly all cases this is a bad idea. Insist they remain in place and assure them that they will be more help there than out in the woods. Keep everyone calm and demonstrate self assurance even if you don't feel it. Go over the signaling system again with them so they will recognize what they hear. Assure them you *will* return even if you don't know how long it will be. Appoint someone to be in charge while you are away. Ensure they understand what you want done and they are capable of doing it. Leave instructions with your appointed leader for a signal to you that would indicate that the lost person had returned while you are out searching.

Question members of the party about the lost person. They may know something that will help give you a starting point. Impress upon them that no bit of information is too small or irrelevant and that it may give you insight into the lost person's state of mind prior to his/her becoming lost. The person may have just wanted to be by him/herself for a while and is not lost at all. They may have been very intent on getting a photo of a moose or other animal or bird and followed it into the woods. One of the members will, in all probability, be the one who saw the lost person last.

There may be circumstances where a person or persons in your party can be used in the search. In making this decision you must be sure of the person's qualifications and ability to do whatever it is you will assign him or her to do. Quite early in my guiding career I decided I would make use of some young person to accompany me if I ever had to search for a lost person. Here's why. As a result of my military service in and around big tank guns, I suffer from tinnitus, constant ringing in my ears. This condition prevents me from hearing certain sounds, especially high pitched sounds such as a whistle. So, I would take a young person with me and use his or her ears. But, I would *never* let them leave my side.

Your search will start at the place last seen (PLS). Here you should do a quick search (hasty search) for any clues as to the direction the person may have taken, anything that may have been left behind or anything else that indicate the person was there. The PLS and any clues, such as tracks, candy wrappers, broken branches, film boxes or anything unusual should be marked with tape, noted on your map and entered into your GPS. If tracks are found, even for a short distance, note the direction and mark the route with tape as far as they can be followed. Lacking the footprints or other clues at the PLS, you may want to do a small grid search in the area of the PLS looking for clues that will give you a starting point. Use your compass to walk square grids small enough that you can eyeball every inch of ground in the area. All during the hasty search, grid search and thereafter until the person is found, you should be using your voice and the designated signal system trying to make contact. Remember, early on the person is probably not far away.

If a direction of travel of the lost person can be ascertained use your compass to determine the azimuth of travel and make note of it. Continue on that likely route for 20 minutes, or more if you think the terrain warrants it. Use your voice and signals as you go. If there is no response and no more clues as to the lost person's having been there, then you should pause and consider your knowledge of the country and consult your topo map to try and figure the most likely direction or place he or she may have gone. Use all of your outdoor skills to make your plan.

Suppose you knew the lost person was at the PLS to get a photograph of a moose he or she had previously seen there. Then it might make sense that he or she had followed the moose to get the picture. Now your wildlife skills come into play as you look at the map and think about where you think the moose would be most likely to head. If your assumption about the person following the moose was correct then it follows that he or she might be in the most "moosey" place in the vicinity.

Don't assume that the lost person is following your carefully given precautions about what to do if they became lost. After all, they are lost and you gave instructions to prevent that. Use your map and your knowledge of the area to try to figure as many "what-ifs" as possible. That done, follow up on them, checking out the most likely ones first. Again it is important to emphasize that noise, shouting and signaling, is a potent resource. Even just your voice covers a much wider area than your eyes in a wooded area. Use your voice and signal often as you continue your search.

Do not let darkness deter you from continuing your search. Except for the fact that you fear for the state of mind of the lost person, the dark can be your ally. It is easier to follow a straight compass line in the dark and it is also easier to hear distant sounds at night. It will slow you down, but that can be a good thing too because it is important to stop often and listen. If yours is a hunting trip then signal shots at night will almost certainly be the lost person, not another hunter shooting at game.

At some point before the night progresses too far it would be a good idea to return to camp to check on the welfare of the others in your party. This will assure them that you are still OK, are concerned about them and that you know what you are doing. Also, it is possible that your lost person found the way back to camp. Once you know everyone else is OK, make a plan and continue with your search, remembering the relationship of the business card to the newspaper as you expand the search area.

When you have exhausted all of your "what-ifs" based on your knowledge of the area and/or a careful map study it is time to expand your search. Determine the area you want to cover and then determine a set of azimuths to cover that area with a series of parallel legs. In this type of search only three azimuths need be determined; the first leg, the short connecting leg and the second leg which is a back-azimuth of the first leg. The distance between the long legs should be what you determine to be twice the distance that your, and the lost person's, signals can be heard. Upon completion of this type of search you can be fairly certain that the lost person is not in the area or that he/she cannot respond to your signals.

The search pattern will never be as neat and even as shown in the illustration. The terrain will dictate the length of each leg and so they may vary. You need to be flexible as you continue your search. If the search pattern turns up a clue then you may want to change plans and follow up on what you have found. The search pattern illustrated is time consuming and will require a large expenditure of energy by you. For this reason it is undertaken only when you feel you have no alternative as you continue your search.

Suppose at some point in your search you hear that long awaited sound - your lost person is signaling you. What now? Now you immediately use your compass to take an azimuth on the direction of the sound and start moving that way, signaling as you go. Hopefully the lost person will continue returning your

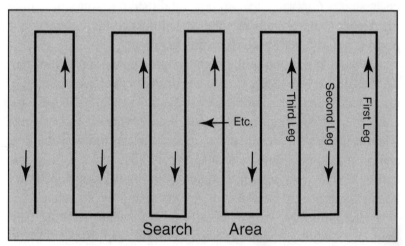

Figure 8 - **A zig-zag search pattern. Only three compass azimuths have to be kept in mind. It is easy to keep track of your progress with map and compass, even easier if you use a GPS too.**

calls and you can zero in on his or her position. Once you find the person you will want to determine that he or she is OK and render any first aid or whatever that is needed. Once satisfied that your guest can travel you will want to return to camp as soon as possible with the good news. With a GPS you can simply punch in a goto for camp and head out on that azimuth with your found person. Lacking a GPS you will probably want to take a back azimuth on the course you used to join the lost person and follow that back to a known point from which you can travel to your camp. Or, you may plot a course with map and compass directly back to camp. Terrain may very well determine the route you use to return - perhaps you know a nearby road that will make night travel back to, or near, your camp much easier that moving through unmarked woods.

Getting Help: If you continue searching without success, there will come a point in time when you will have to call in help. One person cannot go on searching alone indefinitely. For the outdoor leader that time should be when he or she has exhausted the "what ifs" and/or is reaching the limit of his or her own physical ability. When you determine that time has arrived be sure you know the agency you should contact. Have all of the information that you have collected ready for when help arrives. Be prepared to show on the map where you have physically searched, where you have found and marked clues and any other information you may have acquired. It is very possible that you have a better knowledge of the area than the professional(s) there to help you. Also relay all you know about the lost person - age, health, medications used, etc. Your GPS can be a valuable tool in relaying information. Exact coordinates can be given. Be aware though, the GPS is battery operated and could fail at a critical time. Don't depend upon it entirely.

Another electronic device that can be valuable is the cell phone. If contact can be made with one of these then by all means use it. Again, don't depend upon it. It is battery operated - batteries can fail. And, very often areas of outdoor activity are out of range of the nearest cellular tower. If you have contact by cell phone you will be able to call for help at an earlier time than would otherwise be possible. It will also free you from investing the time needed to travel to the nearest land line telephone - time you could be using to continue your search. If you are familiar with the area you are in you will probably know whether or not it is worthwhile carrying a cell phone.

There may be circumstances where a member of your party could be sent to call for help. This can save you a lot of valuable time if it is possible. However, be wary of using this solution. Be very sure that in so doing you do not get another person lost. The lost girl I mentioned earlier was not gone long enough for me to have called in help, but I could have used others in my party to do it. The reason for this was that we were camped across the river from a well used woods road. I could have sent a couple of people across the river by canoe to stop the first car or truck that came along and send word out for help. In the meantime I could have continued searching, secure in the fact that the others could safely cross the river and return. Every circumstance is different - sound judgement needs to be used.

There is no way that you can plan every move ahead of time, but you can plan on the steps you will take and the decisions you will have to make. It is important that you do the advance "what-if" thinking because at the time of a lost person crisis the importance of a clear head is paramount. Your knowledge of the terrain can be your most valuable tool. However, some kinds of outings make it impossible to know the surrounding woods. An example of this would be a river canoe trip or a hiking trip. No one, regardless of how experienced he or she may be, could have detailed knowledge of the miles and miles of woods that would border the river or a hiking trail. In these situations you will have to depend upon good map and compass skills to evaluate the situation and make the best use of your time and energy in the search.

Plan ahead, and like the Boy Scout motto says: **Be Prepared**.

The ✝ Outdoor
Medicine Woman
(or Man)

Medical emergencies are something we don't like to think about, but they are a reality that the outdoor leader must face. The key is to be prepared and then hope that this is where medical experience will rest, not to be called upon while in the field. Like life or medical insurance, no one minds carrying along medical supplies that are never used. Still, the outdoor leader cannot afford to throw a few adhesive strips in his or her pack and call it sufficient preparation. Advanced knowledge of first aid and a complete kit of medical supplies are absolute musts!

I have avoided calling this chapter "First Aid" because first aid is taught with the assumption that the patient can reach a medical professional within 30 minutes or so. Of course, on a wilderness outing this is not possible, and any treatment must be handled accordingly. There are coursed in "Wilderness Medicine" that will prepare the outdoor leader to handle most of the common accidents and illnesses he or she is likely to encounter. If you have the opportunity to take one of those courses it will be to your, and your guests, benefit. However, even though first aid courses are not wholly appropriate for the outdoor person, they are a lot better than nothing. I have taken several and found most of the instructors were willing to make suggestions, beyond calling 911, when I explained what I did.

I will not list the contents of a wilderness medical kit because I feel a person should make up his or her own in accordance with his/her ability to use it. Nor will I try to write a course in wilderness medicine. I recommend you obtain one or more of the following books that will help you to learn to cope with medical emergencies and to make up your own medical kit.

Wilderness Medicine, Beyond First Aid, 5th Edition, by William W. Forgey.

Field Guide to Wilderness Medicine by Paul S. Auerback

Wilderness First Aid: Emergency Care For Remote Locations, National Safety Council

These books are available from amazon.com or they can be ordered for you by most any book store.

My own medical supplies were carried in two kits. The smaller kit was for the usual scrapes, cuts, and abrasions that make up 99 percent of the medical treatment needed on an outdoor expedition. I kept it in my personal pack where it was always handy. When I had teen-agers along, I kept things even handier by filling one of my shirt pockets with a supply of adhesive strips (Band-Aids); I could dispense a dozen or more of them per day. Take plenty!

The larger medical kit contained the more serious supplies, and I kept it in my tool box. This kit was seldom used, so I made a point of checking it at least once per season to be sure everything was still serviceable, up to date, and undamaged. If I used something from the kit, I made a note of it so that I would not forget to replace it as soon as possible.

Part of your advance preparation for an outing is to become aware of any special medical problems of your guests. Be sure to ask them about this so you will know what the problem is and can prepare yourself to administer whatever treatment may be required. If that treatment must be given with an injection, then be sure you are capable of giving one.

People who depend on glasses, particularly those who cannot see without them, should be reminded and urged to carry spares. Glasses are easily dropped and broken or lost. A glasses strap is an excellent precaution.

It is not unusual to have a guest who is allergic to bee stings. That person should have his own kit to take care of the problem, but be sure you know how to use it too, in case the victim is unconscious. Multiple insect stings/bites sometime cause a reaction in some people. Most times this is treated by keeping the victim from further insect stings/bites and keeping him or her under observation until the situation clears up.

The outdoor leader must be aware of the dangers that each season may bring. In the summer the sun may be a factor that your guests are not used to dealing with. They should be warned about sunburn and encouraged to use sunscreen as well as the proper clothing. A fair skinned person can sunburn quickly and it can ruin an outing for him or her as well as others in the group. Also, during hot weather watch your guests for signs of dehydration, sunburn, heat exhaustion and sunstroke. During cold weather be on the lookout for frostbite and in all seasons be aware of the possibility of hypothermia. All of these weather-related conditions are covered in detail in the Weather chapter.

I get an annual physical exam by my doctor. He reminds me yearly that we are practicing preventive medicine. I recommend anyone who is responsible for others do the same thing. Not give them a physical, but take proactive steps to prevent any medical emergency that it is possible to prevent.

Preventive medicine (so to speak) has worked for me. There have been only two incidents in over 30 years that I consider serious. And, only one that required medical evacuation. She broke her ankle while running across a dirt road to get a photograph. The other was a teen-ager who somehow hooked his cheek while fishing. I had to cut the fish hook out with a razor blade. His parents were there and gave permission for the "operation". Antiseptics were used and the incision was nearly healed by the end of the trip.

When I was a small boy, the radio was to us what TV is to kids today. We each had programs we listened to regularly, and one of my favorites was a short one called *The Story Man*. Each weekday morning, before school, he told a five-minute story and then signed off with a safety slogan: "Always alert, never get hurt." With these words ringing in my ears every morning, I kissed my mother goodbye and dashed out to catch the school bus.

"Always alert, never get hurt" - it must have made a deep impression on me as a boy growing up in rural Maine, because it still comes to mind sixty-odd years later. It is good advice and I've tried to follow it. When you think about accidents, or hear about them, you see that a good many of them are caused by inattention. The outdoor leader has to be constantly alert to the hazards that may threaten the safety of the people in his or her care. Your knowledge of the country you are in, and of the up-coming activities, will allow you to formulate plans to deal with any dangers that may be faced. Whatever your outdoor activity, your mind should be at least one day ahead of where you are. I had a situation on a canoe trip that required firm decision making and also diplomacy. I include it here because I have always felt that the decision prevented injury to one or more of my party.

My party was a group of middle aged men. Though I tried several times, I could not get them to practice the canoe strokes I knew they would need for the rapids that were coming up. The day before we would get to the rapids I announced that I we wouldn't run them, but would portage instead. I said I felt there was a real danger of upsetting and losing or damaging gear. They were disappointed, but had no choice but to accept my decision - I made that clear. I didn't mention the fact that they failed to respond to my several requests for whitewater training sessions, but I suspect they understood.

Several days later one of their canoes upset in *very* easy rapids, Class I. That evening as we sat around the campfire one of the men said to me, "you were right back there", meaning the enforced portage. It made me feel better, but either way I knew I was right.

If you have a situation similar to mine, be firm. You tell them, "We cannot run this white water," not: "We might be able to make it, but maybe we'd better not."

I can think of nothing so satisfying as helping a handicapped person in an outdoor excursion. It is an experience that such a person could never hope to have except in the company of a responsible, woods wise person. If you ever have such an opportunity, I highly recommend it - the adventure may well do you more good than it does the person you are responsible for!

One member of a group of young people I guided on a river trip was legally blind. I got to know him quite well before the trip and I was impressed with his positive attitude toward life and the future. He was realistic, and we openly discussed his problem and the trip we were going to undertake. I also talked with his mother, who, though worried, was supportive and anxious for him to have the experience.

I made the boy the bow paddler in my canoe, and he was a good one. He couldn't see the rocks when we ran white water, but he was well coordinated and would respond instantly to my commands, drawing right or left without hesitation. I remember him yelling to me, as we started down our first rapids of the trip, "I can't see the rocks, but you tell me what to do and I'll do it." He did too. We never touched a rock, and in our cooperation, quite a camaraderie built up between us. As a group member he pulled his own weight, doing camp chores every bit as well as anyone else. Years later I got a call from him and learned he had a full time job, was married and had two children. This confirmed my conviction that he would pull his own weight through life.

I told the above story, with a few more details, in a magazine where I wrote a monthly column. One day, a couple of years after publication of the story, I got a telephone call that brought tears to my eyes. The man on the other end of the line told me his name and then told me that he had just then returned home from his daughter's funeral. He called to thank me for writing the story because it had encouraged him to take his handicapped daughter on a canoe trip. That canoe trip turned out to be the high point of her short life.

Each handicapped person must be considered according to his or her particular problems. Very often the problems are multiple, but do consider taking someone on a outing if you have the opportunity. If it is feasible, then by all means do it. You'll never regret it.

Hunting & Fishing

The highest praise that can be given to a leader by those who he/she has led is that the leader never asks them to do anything he/she wouldn't do. This concept holds true with the outdoor leader. You have to have "been there, done that" before you can lead others in hunting and fishing. The knowledge you must posses only comes from enthusiastically engaging in the activity yourself for number of years. Even if you are confidant of your abilities you will find you have much to learn and that the learning will come over the years of experience with others in the field. What I will try to do in this chapter is point out some of the mistakes others have made and some of the experiences that have made them better outdoor leaders.

A common mistake by new leaders is their assumption that their guests have the skills necessary to take game or fish and that all the leader has to do is to show them where to go. Guests very often claim to more experience than they actually have. However, as an accomplished hunter or fisherman, the leader can spot their inexperience in short order. My friend Dick Mosher tells a couple of stories that illustrate how wrong it is to assume the guests are as accomplished as they may seem at first meeting.

Dick guides bear hunters in early fall in Maine. The hunts are from baited stands. When the hunters arrive at the camp for their week's hunt, usually on Sunday, it is the common practice to have them fire their rifles at a target before heading out for the hunt on Monday. The target is usually a paper plate with a black aiming point in the center. It is located 30 yards from the shooter, the usual distance from the stand to the bear bait. They fire from a rest because the purpose is to check the accuracy of the rifle, not the hunters shooting skill, although that will become apparent in any case.

One of his hunters arrived with a brand new .30-06 caliber Smith & Wesson rifle with a Nikon scope, an expensive outfit. After the hunter missed the target twice, Dick asked if he could give it a try. He hit the plate dead center. Next, Dick told the hunter he was going to put an expended cartridge in the rifle and for him to aim and fire again. At the click of the rifle, the hunter's problem was immediately apparent. He was closing his eyes and flinching badly when he pulled the trigger, even though he *knew* the rifle wouldn't fire. It was then the hunter admitted that, until that Sunday, he had *never fired a firearm before in his life!*

Out of respect and concern for the animal they would be hunting, Dick would not allow the hunter go to a stand. Instead he spent all his spare time in the following days instructing the hunter and helping him learn how to shoot. By Thursday the hunter was sufficiently skilled that he was allowed to start his bear hunt.

One summer one of Dick's guests arrived at camp to do some fly fishing. After meeting the man and talking for a while Dick learned that the man had been fly fishing for five years. An experienced guest is always good news to a guide, but when they headed out to go fishing Dick noticed the handle of the man's fly rod looked brand new - clean and relatively unused. "Oh, I see you have a new rod", said Dick. "No", replied the man, "I've had this one for five years".

From this bit of information it was apparent that the man was

Judy Mosher photo

Photo 31 - **Sighting in. It is important to ensure firearms are right on before starting the hunt. It prevents misses and, more importantly, helps prevent wounded game.**

not an experienced fly fisherman, and would need patient instruction if he was to catch fish with that brand new, five year old fly rod.

An outdoor leader will usually have an idea of the success of a hunt or a fishing trip as soon as it is over, but the best indication may take a year or more to surface. It is this. If the guest is on a hunt and does not shoot the animal being hunted, or if the fisherman fails to net fish it may seem to a young guide that the trip was a failure. But, if after this apparent failure the same guest appears the following year, then the leader can be proud that he or she has done a good job, and that in spite of the lack of game the guest had a good time. There is more to outdoor leadership than the shooting and fishing.

Show and tell about things that are common place to you in the environment you know. An example here in Maine could be to show the remarkable qualities of birch bark as a fire starter, even when wet. Or, how to find and chew spruce gum. Also, there are also stories that can be told to fill in the times of inactivity. This all brings up the difference between hunting and shooting, and between fishing and catching.

If a hunter just wants to shoot animals he may as well go to game farm where the animals can be observed going by and selected animals can be shot. If a fisherman just wants to catch fish there are commercial ponds where stocked fish are there ready and willing to grab the first bit of food presented to them on a hook. These activities should not be confused with hunting and fishing where one takes his or her chances on the possibility of success. Most outdoor leaders understand this difference and the successful ones are able to convey the concept to most of their guests.

If you, as a leader, are going to take people, unknown to you, on a hunt or fishing trip, it is important that you find out something about them and that they understand what you will and will not do. A controversial subject in Maine is the hunting method of driving deer. After being illegal for a period of time it is again legal for a maximum of three hunters to drive. Many of us do not agree with this practice and refuse to participate in such a hunt. It is important for a guest to know ahead of time that you will not drive deer, because such a hunt may be common practice where the guest comes from.

What the guest will be using for a firearm is important to know. The leader should have standards of his own that are equal to or more stringent than the law allows. Although bear is a valued and respected game animal in Maine it is still legal to hunt them with absolutely any firearm right down to, and including, a .22-short. Maybe someday this shortcoming in our laws will be corrected, but that is how it stands today. A guide that used only the law as his/her standard would be doing this game animal a great disservice.

A serious mistake made by some guides is to shoot an animal while guiding hunters or to catch more fish than the person she/he is guiding. This is almost certain to cause hard feelings and should be carefully avoided. In my service on Maine's Guide Board, I have heard more complaints about this practice than any other. Of course, this practice is not against the law, so does not come under our aegis. Nevertheless, it is upsetting to hear complaints like this because a bad light reflects on all of us.

Dick tells this story on himself. He does not do it proudly, but in his defense I should say that he was much younger and inexperienced at the time. He was guiding a hunter on a bobcat hunt with a dog. These hunts are in the dead of winter in Maine and the days are short. As darkness approached, Dick was anxious to get his dog and head out of the woods. It isn't easy to get a good hunting dog away from the chase so when the bobcat came running by, Dick took the opportunity to get his dog - by shooting the cat.

Dick's hunter was a very capable hunter and handled the situation with class. Still, he managed to let his feelings be known when he said, "I thought *I* was the hunter." This is recalled by Dick as one of the most humiliating and humbling experiences in his years of guiding and one he vows will never be allowed to happen again. We must learn from our mistakes. You have the chance to learn from someone else's!

When out fishing, the guest often invites the guide to go ahead and fish. Dick does not refuse this invitation, but instead uses it as a time of experimentation. If fly fishing, he will try different flies until one works out really well, then he will have his guest use it. In this way he continues to learn more about fly fishing and his guest gets to catch fish - the reason they are both there in the first place. Dick will then continue experimenting to ensure that he doesn't out-fish his guest.

Often in guiding hunters it becomes necessary for the guide to track wounded animals. Here again it is important that the guide not do the shooting when the time comes to finish off the game. Even with dangerous animals such as bear or large cats, it is always best to allow the guest to deliver the killing shot. The guide can always stand by with his rifle ready if the situation develops that will put the guest, or the guide, in danger. Of course, the safety of the guest should always be uppermost in the leader's mind, so common sense has to prevail.

The tools of the trade for the outdoor leader are the rods,

reels, line, etc. of the fisherman or the firearms and ammunition, bows and arrows, etc. of the hunter. It is important that the guide have some knowledge of these things because the guests will expect it. This is not to say that the leader can be an expert in every aspect of his sport, but he or she has to have a working knowledge.

The hunting guide has to understand ballistics, know how to sight in a variety of firearms, and also be able to give instruction where needed. An example of the kind of knowledge needed is this ballistic fact that confuses many people, but should be common knowledge to a hunting leader. When shooting downhill a rifle will shoot slightly high - it depends on the angle how high. Many do not realize that the same is true when shooting uphill - the rifle will shoot high! There's not room for a lengthy explanation here, but if you doubt it, check it out.

Some knowledge of black powder firearms and of archery equipment is also necessary. The fishing guide needs to understand what equipment will be needed to accomplish what her/his guest is there to do. It may be necessary to furnish what is needed if the guest shows up ill-equipped.

It has been pointed out in other parts of this book, but it is important to stress it again here that what the guest wants and expects should be given careful consideration by the outdoor leader. Some will simply say, "you're the guide, you decide." Others will have certain expectations that may or may not be possible to meet. The guide should meet the expectations that are possible and diplomatically explain why others cannot be met while at the same time offering some appealing alternatives. It is always best if as many of these decisions as possible can be made before the guest arrives. That way there are no disappointments or unreasonable expectations.

The hunting or fishing outdoor leader must have a passion for the sport before considering leading others. Further, the guide must be of the mind that the success of the guests is how his or her success is measured. If the guide can take satisfaction from that concept she/he will be successful, and if not then he or she has no business guiding others in any activity.

On becoming a
Professional

To become a professional guide the most obvious requirement is that the person be skilled in the outdoor activity he or she plans to lead people into. That is a given, but there are some qualities that the guide must possess if he or she is to be successful.

It is a people business - it is about dealing with people. Most of the time you will like those people because they have an interest in things you are interested in, otherwise they would not have hired you in the first place. There will be the occasional exception though, and you must be willing, and able, to smile and treat the offensive individual just as you would anyone else. There will be times when your judgement is called to question, when your decision does not quite agree with what the guest thinks should happen. Then you need to bring your experience and diplomacy into play and convince them your decision is sound. If you cannot, then you must be able to be firm and stick to your decision in spite of their displeasure.

The rewards will be many as you help people do what you love to do and show them places where you love to go. There is also great satisfaction in running a small business of your own.

If you decide to turn professional, take money for your services, you will probably continue to do the same things you did when you were just one of the group who happened to take charge. But, you are going into business, and as a business person you will have responsibilities that you didn't even have to think about before. You will have to decide what to charge, how to advertise your services and learn to keep accurate financial records. And there will need to be a whole array of policies that will govern your relationship with your guests. A couple of things must be taken care of right from the moment you make the decision to go pro. One is to be sure you are legal. In my state one must hold a guides license, issued by the state, if he/she gets paid for services. Some states do not even have guides, so it is something that you must check out before accepting money for your services. The other, that can be very important to you, is the matter of liability.

Liability Insurance: I have heard some young guides remark that they didn't need to worry too much about liability because they had little or nothing to lose. I'm not a lawyer, but it seems to me that a judgement against someone can be against future earnings. So, if a young person is ordered by the court to pay, say $100,000, that judgement remains in effect until the payment is complete. In this case, then, the young guide has plenty to lose because the judgement is not dropped just because the money is not immediately available. Because of this, it is imperative that anyone guiding people on any outdoor expedition, for pay, should acquire liability insurance.

It is not always easy for a professional guide to find insurance. What guides do seems to be considered extremely dangerous by those who make the decisions from behind their desks, in offices, high above the streets, in some far off city. A few years ago an insurance agent, friendly to guides in the state of Maine, did a survey of insurance claims against guides. He found none! Zero! Yet, the cost for liability insurance remains very high and has to be purchased for an entire year in spite of the fact that most guides operate on a seasonal basis, usually only two to six months a year.

The first place to look for guide's liability insurance is a professional association. If your state has one check with them to see if they offer a group insurance for members. Even if they do not, they can advise you where and how their members are insured. If you have to go directly to an insurance agent you may have to look around. Start with your agent that takes care of your other insurance needs (auto, house, etc.) My agent was enthusiastic about taking care of all my insurance needs (He already had my cars and my homeowners insurance). I told him I doubted if he could improve in on what I already had, but to go ahead and check. He came back a few days later and said I had better stick with my group policy with the Maine Professional Guides Association. He not only couldn't save me any money, but could not even find a carrier among the companies he used that would issue a policy.

It may not be entirely your decision whether or not you carry liability insurance. It could be a requirement of the government body that issues your license or it could be a requirement of the landowners on whose land you will be operating. In Maine much of the wild land is regulated by an organization of landowners called North Maine Woods. This organization operates all gates and collects fees. It brings order out of the chaos that existed when each landowner made its own rules and set its own fees. North Maine Woods requires guides operating on their lands to have a commercial permit. To obtain the commercial permit the guide must show proof of liability insurance.

Before I leave this unpleasant matter of insurance I will complicate your life a little more. If you use your vehicle to transport your guests to or from whatever activity you are conducting, you should have commercial insurance on your vehicle. Some rationalize that they are being paid for the guiding, not the transportation. If the insurance company will buy into that rationale then all is well and good. But, you had better be sure! My own solution to this problem, on my guided canoe trips, was to transport gear in my truck, but not people. I had the people use their own vehicles and I arranged for them to be transported by a licensed, insured transporter to the scheduled take-out point.

Assumption of Risk: This statement goes along with the liability insurance. Some insurance companies will insist the insured have guests sign a statement similar to the one shown in Photo 32. Yours can be modified to cover the kind of situation you will be undertaking. Whether or not you are required by your insurance company to do so, it is a good idea to have your guests sign an assumption of risk statement just so they know what the possible risks are in whatever it is you are about to undertake with them.

If possible have the guests sign the statement before they arrive. Send them out with your correspondence with a stamped, self-addressed envelope to ensure its return in a timely manner. If they don't get to see the statement until they arrive, and if the worst happens, the injured party may claim he/she didn't realize the risk until the last minute and then felt it was too late to back out. I never had anyone object to signing the Assumption of Risk statement.

As can be seen the statement can also be used as a guest registration. This gives you an opportunity to get information in writing that may be vital at some point later on. Each adult in your party should sign one and parents can include minor children on their registration. I always carried copies of each signed statement with me on my trips for reference in case of an emergency.

Business Decisions: One of the first things a new business person has to face is how to bring in business. This can be hard for the new guide because he has no professional experience to hold up for proof of competency. A good way to get valuable professional experience is to work for an established guide, or sporting camp. Be aware right away however, of the ethical problems that can come up. Your employer certainly will be. You must be extremely careful not to in any way seem to be trying to lure your employer's guests away and to your own budding busi-

Gil Gilpatrick
P.O. Box 461
Skowhegan, ME 04976
GUEST REGISTRATION AND ACKNOWLEDGEMENT

Name:_____ Phone:_____

Home Address: _____

_____

Names of minor children included in this registration:

_____

***

List of any special medical needs for you or minor members of your family accompanying you:

_____

Person to notify in the event of an emergency:

Name:_____ Phone:_____

Address:_____

ASSUMPTION OF RISK STATEMENT

    I, (We), the undersigned, am (are) about to take a canoe camping trip into the Maine backwoods and waters with Volney (Gil) Gilpatrick of Fairfield, Maine.

    I, (We) understand that such a trip involves considerable risk of injury or loss, (including, but not limited to: loss of property or life from overturned or swamped canoes which may result from many different causes such as inexperience in handling a canoe, hazardous white water, illness from drinking untreated water, exertion from portages, motor vehicle accident in transit, hyperthermia from immersion in cold water, lightning, lack of communication or unavailability of early medical treatment).

    AS PART OF THE CONSIDERATION FOR THE SERVICES TO BE RENDERED, (I), (WE) THE UNDER-SIGNED, AND ON BEHALF OF OURSELVES, FAMILY, HEIRS, PERSONAL REPRESENTATIVES, AND MINOR MEMBERS OF OUR FAMILY ACCOMPANYING US, FURTHER RELEASE AND HOLD HARMLESS, VOLNEY (GIL) GILPATRICK, HIS AGENTS, EMPLOYEES, AND ASSOCIATES, FROM ANY AND ALL LIABILITY, CAUSES OF HIS ACTIONS, CLAIMS AND DEMANDS WHICH MAY ARISE OUT OF THE ABOVE EXPEDITION.

    (I), (WE), HAVE READ THIS AGREEMENT AND UNDERSTAND ITS CONTENT AND PURPOSE. AFTER FULL CONSIDERATION OF ALL THE ABOVE, (I), (WE) HEREBY ASSUME ALL RISKS OF INJURY OR LOSS WHICH (I), (WE) MIGHT SUFFER DURING THE ABOVE CANOE CAMPING TRIP OR ANY OTHER ACTIVITY TO BE ARRANGED BY OR TO BE TAKEN WITH VOLNEY (GIL) GILPATRICK.

Dated:_____

Signed:_____

Photo 32 - **This Assumption of Risk statement can be easily adapted to just about any guiding business. It ensures that the guide and guest understand each other in all aspects of the upcoming outing.**

ness. A friend of mine, Master Guide, Dick Mosher, does a lot of guiding for a sporting camp. He has set a rigid set of ethics for himself that ensures he will continue to be a trusted and valued guide as long as he wishes to do so.

Dick will not accept a job from one of the camp's guests regardless of how well he knows the person or how much the guest may plead for him to do so. When the services the guest is requesting are *not* offered by the camp, Dick still does what needs to be done to keep things on the up and up. He will tell the camp owner what he is being asked to do. Of course he has the owners blessings, because it takes no business away from the camp, and you can be sure he has the owners complete trust for his efforts.

If a guide fails to adhere to strict ethical standards he/she will soon have a hard time finding work. Camp owners and guides make up a very small fraternity. They all know each other, and the word spreads fast.

Any business person will agree that word-of-mouth is the most valuable form of advertising. Of course you have to get started somewhere. When I was getting started I gained valuable experience and made a lot of good contacts, by contracting trips with summer camps. I only needed to deal with one person, the camp director. Through him, and the enthusiastic kids who went home talking to their parents about their great trip, my name became known to people who would never have heard of it otherwise. Look around for possibilities that will fit your business plan.

Another thing that helped me get started was writing. I wrote a canoe column for a regional outdoor magazine, as well as some books. Many of the stories I wrote described situations I was involved in as a guide, and so I was recognized, justifiably or not, as an expert in my field. I signed up many people who first learned my name through my writing. If you have a flair, and interest in writing, look into it. It has its own rewards (financial being one of the lesser ones) and gives a lot of name recognition.

Advertising can be an expensive process for a small business. It is especially hard for a guide because most of the services he offers has to draw on a national audience. Here again a professional association can help out. Not only will there be other professionals who will share advice, but there will be listings that will include your name and specialty. Many professional associations advertise nationally for their members so the listing, with your name on it, will get exposure that you as an individual could not afford.

The Internet has made it possible for the individual entrepreneur to get the same exposure as a multi-million dollar corporation. The only problem is you have to get your URL (Uniform Resource Locator) to the attention of an interested party. This brings us back to the expensive problem of advertising. You have probably noticed that just about all of the big corporations advertise their URL on national television and anywhere else they spend money to attract customers. The guide running a one-person business cannot do the same national advertising as the large corporation, but he or she can be sure that the URL is on whatever advertising that is possible. This can include letterheads, business cards, brochures, ads and anything else that is printed for distribution.

Don't overlook classified advertising. In the right publication it can bring in a lot of inquiries with a relatively small expenditure. Even a small classified ad may seem very expensive in a national magazine, but in advertising you get what you pay for, and people do read those classified ads. You pay for most classified advertising by the word with, usually, a minimum number or words. You can keep the expense down by omitting your mailing address and giving only your phone number and URL. In most publications these each only count as one word. Do include your name or the name of your business, however, not just the service you are offering.

It is important to realize that advertising is a long term affair. Don't expect a huge immediate response. I have signed up customers who first saw my ad, or however they found me, two or three years previous, so don't count the ad as a failure right away. It may go something like this: They see your small classified ad. They request and get your brochure. After looking it over they decide it is something they would like to do when the kids are two or three years older. Out of the blue, three years later, you sign up someone who you have long forgotten ever having contact with.

Develop a Brochure: As a commercial guide you will need
a brochure which will attractively display your services to anyone interested enough to request it. The size will depend upon
the amount of material you have to put in it, but make it so it can
be mailed either by itself or in a business size envelope. Your
printer can help you with the brochure, or if you have the computer and necessary software and hardware you can produce your
own.

The brochure should use as many photos as possible which
show what you do and the area(s) you do it in. It is also important
to have a photo of you, preferable engaged in some activity related to your business. You will probably want to go with all
black and white because color is very expensive to produce for
the small business person. I did not feel I could afford color even
after many years of successful operation.

Like most information pieces, the brochure should tell who,
what, where and when. Along with your photo, tell about yourself and why your are the best person for them to hire. You have
to walk a fine line here to present yourself in the best possible
light without sounding like an egotistical braggart. Give your
experience; it doesn't matter that it was not commercial guiding
experience, but don't try to claim something you do not honestly
understand or have accomplished. People will also be interested
in the food, what they have to bring, the experience level needed
(if any) and how to go about booking with you.

Be aware that people order brochures, especially free ones,
for anything they see or hear about that interests them. Like with
other types of advertising, don't expect immediate response when
you mail out a brochure. They are a long-term affair.

Unless you are producing your brochures in small quantities,
you will probably want to avoid including your prices because
they are always subject to change. A good alternative is to make
up a separate price sheet that can be easily produced with a copier
and include it with each brochure you send out. The reverse side
of the price sheet could serve as a sign up sheet for the customer
to use in booking.

Maine Wilderness Canoe Vacations

with

Gil Gilpatrick

Gil Gilpatrick
P.O. Box 461
Skowhegan, Maine 04976
(207) 453-6959

"Look here! (said the Water Rat.) "If you've really nothing else on hand this morning, supposing we drop down the river together, and have a long day of it?"

The mole waggled his toes from sheer happiness, spread his chest with a sigh of full contentment, and leaned back blissfully into the soft cushions. "What a day I'm having!" he said, "Let us start at once!"

Kenneth Grahame,
The Wind In The Willows

Photo 33 - **This is the outside of the brochure I used for many years. It measured 8 1/2" X 16" and was printed on both sides. Folded, it could be mailed as-is or placed into a business size envelope.**

Dealing with People: Every once in a while there can be a "Trip from Hell" for anyone who is in the guiding business. It can happen, but don't bring it on yourself.

Your guests are hiring you to show them the best way to do the activity. They are hiring you to take care of them and see them safely through to the scheduled end of the activity. With these things in mind do not allow them to make decisions that are contrary to you doing your job. This is the place where your skills as a diplomat come into play. You have to convince them that your way is the best way without your seeming to be an unfeeling dictator.

One of the things that frequently caused raised eyebrows with people on my canoe trips was my announcement that everyone would be rousted out of bed by 6 AM if they weren't up before. I insisted on an early start and had several good reasons for it. I never asked them what time they wanted to get up, except for a lay-over day (a day we would not travel). I did follow up the announcement with the several good reasons for it. It usually took two or three days, but almost always someone would come up to me and remark what a good system this "start early" thing was. If you have something you think is important then present it to your guests as if it is the way it *has* to be done. If you feel that strongly about it then you have reasons. Tell them the reasons. However, if there are choices that are not important to the overall success of the trip, then let the guests have a choice. They will appreciate it and feel they are contributing to the experience. (They will be!)

Most of the time you will be dealing with people who have interests similar to your own, otherwise they wouldn't have hired you. Because of this you will have a lot in common with them and will sincerely like nearly all of them. There will be the occasional exception, and you will be asking yourself, *why is this guy here?* You will probably never find out, but you will have to put that aside and do your best to see that he has as good a time as possible. I remember one I had who, I was sure, must have had a terrible time. Call him Harry. He seemed surly, unhappy and out of place for the whole trip. From my point of view, nothing seemed to go right for Harry. A couple of years later I had a guest who said he signed on with me because Harry had recommended me. Go figure, huh?

Set out any ground rules you can ahead of time so there will not be any misunderstanding. If you think something you consider important might not set well with all or some of your guests after the trip starts, then bring it up ahead of time so no one has anything to complain about later. (I always did with my "start early" edict). There will be unexpected situations that will need a decision by you. You must always use your experience in making your decision, keeping in mind your responsibility for the well being of your guests. *Their safety is your number one priority!* If you see more than one solution, that is the time to allow a democratic choice.

Money Matters: A beginning guide working for a sporting camp or another guide will probably have to be content in accepting whatever the employer decides is a fair wage, at least in the beginning. If you are a guide starting up your own business it is hard to know just how much to charge. As a business person you should consider a number of factors to come up with a fair and profitable amount.

Start out by figuring, as closely as possible, how much it will cost you to conduct the activity you propose to do. There is a tendency, and a temptation, to stop there and count anything you get above those costs as profit. If you plan to be in this business for the long-haul don't do that. You may already own some, if not all, of the equipment you need. But, that equipment was not free and it will not last forever, especially with the increased use you plan to give it. Figure in an amount that will eventually allow you to replace your equipment (whether you ever do, or not).

Now you need to decide how much you should receive as wages for each day you will be acting as guide. It helps to do this if you know the going rate for guides working for someone else. In arriving at this figure you must remember that you will spend a considerable amount of time preparing for the activity as well as time cleaning up and repairing equipment after the activity is over. Also, even if yours is a seasonal activity, you will spend a considerable amount of time through the year planning your advertising, corresponding with prospects, and sending out brochures. All of this time, and the material involved, ultimately has to be paid for by your guests if your business is to be successful.

Above and beyond what you are paid as your own employee, should be a profit. Profit is not a dirty word - it is the American way. It is what drives our economy. If you are going to be satisfied with just earning wages, why put up with the hassle of running your own business? Work for someone else and let them do the worrying.

After considering all of the things I have mentioned, and possibly more, it helps your own peace of mind to find out what others in the same business are doing. I did this in my early years. I had someone else request brochures and prices so I didn't have to use my own name. Sneaky maybe, but some people are not anxious to help others get started. I am sure others have done the same thing with me in my thirty-plus years in business. When asked, I willingly helped others starting out by honestly telling what I charged and how I arrived at it. There is always a temptation by someone just starting out to undercut on prices to attract business. Eventually that person will have to come up to the level of others, so the sooner you make them realize that, the better off everyone in the business will be.

Beware of people looking for freebies! As an outdoor writer as well as a guide, I became aware of this thing early on. Some outdoor writers (some self proclaimed) will try to wrangle a free outing with a guide on the pretense of writing up the experience and thus giving the guide exposure he could never otherwise afford. For sure, exposure in a national or even regional, magazine will help a guide's career in many ways.

If the writer is on the up and up he will show evidence that he has been hired by a magazine to do the story. You can check it out. If it turns out that he is free-lancing, hoping to sell the story, the situation is different. If the writer is up front about the situation you might offer a reduced rate or even a freebie if you wish. But, if he is not completely truthful, leave it alone. Walk away! I have had writers and photographers from national magazines do three major stories about me and my service. In every case the magazines paid the full price for the professionals to be on my guided trip - they expected as much. I have to admit that, after seeing the multi-page, full color articles, I felt kind of guilty about charging them. But, too late by then.

Don't forget that as a business person you have a record keeping responsibility. The IRS insists on it! Initially you will just

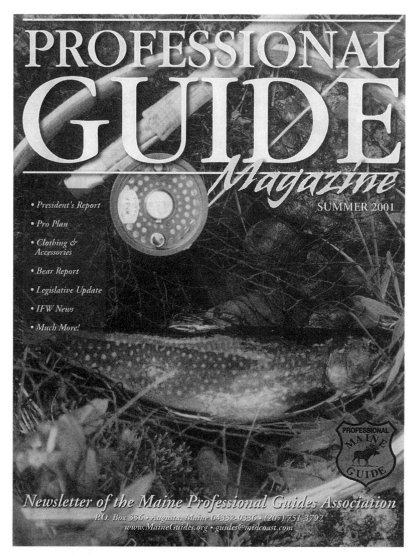

Photo 34 - **Membership in a professional organization can be of great benefit to a guide, especially one just getting started.**

need to keep track of business related expenses and income. As your business grows so will your record keeping, so take it one step at a time. I keep careful records, but I rely on an accountant to do my tax returns. As long as I furnish her accurate information, she will keep me out of trouble with the government. Another benefit is having someone to consult whenever I am unsure of something tax related. Consider hiring a professional unless you know you have the skills to do the various forms that may be needed by the IRS.

Guiding is a people business. For sure, you need the outdoor skills to even consider going into it, but they are secondary to the real job of caring for people in the out-of-doors.

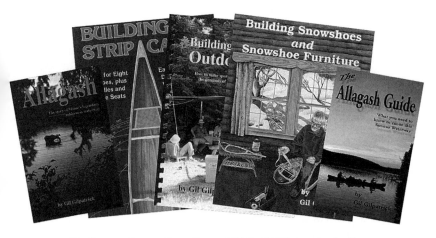

Other books by Gil Gilpatrick:

Allagash, The story of Maine's legendary wilderness Waterway
Quality paperback, 6"X9", 235 pages $15.00

Building A Strip Canoe, Easy step by step instructions for 8
canoe models, plus half size patterns.
Quality paperback, 8 1/2 X 11", 128 pages $11.95

Building Outdoor Gear, How to make sporting equipment that
will meet the demands of the serious outdoor person.
Comb-bound, 8 1/2" X 11", 115 pages $13.95

Building Snowshoes and Snowshoe Furniture, Plans and
instructions to build 5 snowshoe models and 5 pieces of furniture.   Quality paperback, 8 1/2" X 11", 160 pages $19.95

The Allagash Guide, What you need to know to canoe this
famous Waterway.
Quality paperback, 5 1/2" X 8 1/2", 88 pages $11.95

Order from: Gil Gilpatrick   Tel: 207-453-6959
             P.O. Box 461   Fax: 207-238-9243
             Skowhegan, ME 04976

Order on line at: www.gilgilpatrick.com
MasterCard, Visa

(Add $2.50 for shipping for all titles. May combine 2 for $2.50)